Presented to:

_____

Presented by:

_____

Date:

_____

God's Little Devotional Book for Couples

Special Gift Edition

Honor Books
Tulsa, Oklahoma

Introduction

SIMPLIFY. That's the buzzword these days. How many of us, however, are really doing it? And once we do, what benefits are we reaping? What are we doing with our newly found time? Are we spending it with our families, or are we filling it up with other activities?

This new edition of *God's Little Devotional Book for Couples* has been condensed and simplified from the original to provide you with the best advice, stories, quotes, and thought-provoking questions about marriage and family. The beauty of this new volume will draw you to pick it up on a regular basis. The artwork alone is worth flipping through the pages. But once you're captured by the artwork, the quotes and scriptures will intrigue you. Then, before you know it, you'll have read several devotions.

Share the insights and stories with your spouse. And practice the things you've learned. Use your simplified lifestyle as a means to building a stronger family—a stronger relationship with your spouse and a stronger relationship with your children. *God's Little Devotional Book for Couples* will inspire and encourage you toward that end. Spend some time reading it today!

The family begins in a commitment of love.

IF you were to hold a lump of dark green clay in one hand and a lump of light green clay in the other, you could clearly identify the two shades of color. However, if you were to mold the two lumps together, kneading them thoroughly, you would see just one lump of green clay—at least at first glance.

Upon closer inspection, you could see the separate lines of dark and light green clay, yet it would be virtually impossible to separate the clay into two pure colors again.

That is an image of what it means for a husband and wife to become "one flesh." Love binds the couple together, especially as they knead out some of their differences and develop a life of mutual goals, activities, and relationships.

A grandma once told her young granddaughter that Jim and June were coming for a visit. With eager anticipation, they baked special treats and cleaned the house thoroughly in expectation of their overnight stay. Upon their arrival the little girl exclaimed with wide-eyed wonder, "Nanna, there are two people. Someone came with Jim-and-June!" Just like the well-blended clay, in marriage we are no longer two, but one.

For this reason a man shall leave his father and his mother and shall be joined to his wife, and the two shall become one flesh.

Ephesians 5:31 AMP

A personal relationship with Jesus Christ is the cornerstone of marriage.

8

MARRIAGE involves a blending of lives, not merely a "joining." Many marriages flounder because each spouse continues to look back over their shoulder at freedoms and relationships they had in the past. When a couple invites Jesus Christ to be the cornerstone of their marriage—the strong foundation upon which they build their relationship—they are inviting Him to walk before them. Then He is free to lead them forward into the unique purpose He has for them *as a married couple.*

We are unique as individuals, but each marriage is also unique. It is as individual and one-of-a-kind as the two people involved. Just as God created us as completely original individuals, so we need to invite Him to make our marriages completely original relationships. This can only happen when each person in the relationship yields his or her individuality to God's higher purpose.

C. S. Lewis said, "Self exists to be abdicated. In self-giving we touch a rhythm, not only of all creation, but of all being, for the Eternal Word also gives Himself in sacrifice."

Marriage was designed to teach us about our love relationship with Jesus. The key to a good marriage is loving self-sacrifice.

Behold I lay in Zion a choice stone, a precious corner stone, and he who believes in Him shall not be disappointed.

1 Peter 2:6

The most important thing a father can do for his children is to love their mother.

WASHINGTON POST columnist William Raspberry wrote a loving tribute to his wife, seemingly unaware that he was reflecting his own role in her success: "The second Sunday in May was not just Mother's Day for our family—it was Mother's Graduation Day, one of the great moments in our household.

"My wife, Sondra, was one of those 'responsible' young women who decided after high school to spare her family the economic burden of college and go directly to work. Then she got married, and her family became her first priority.

"I don't know precisely what made her decide to go back to school. . . . It wasn't easy, studying part-time while managing the lives of a husband and three children. . . .

"On graduation day, it was announced that she had been inducted into both the adult honor society and Phi Beta Kappa. The kids shrieked as though she had won the Nobel Prize for Smart Moms. Some people may have trouble understanding how we could get excited about something as routine as a bachelor's degree. But if you have ever taken up something difficult and made a howling success of it, you'll understand why we are so proud."

Husbands, love your wives, as Christ loved the church and gave Himself up for her.
❧ Ephesians 5:25 AMP ❧

Love is being willing to face the risks of seeing your spouse's dreams come true.

IN their book, *My Lover, My Friend,* Colleen and Louis Evans Jr. write: "David and Nancy Low are one of the most exciting young couples we have met since coming to Washington. He is a financial lawyer, and she is a top-flight public relations administrator. . . .

"After working in another state for a well-known and respected political leader, Nancy was offered a very high position in a federal government agency. This opportunity was made even more exciting by the fact that it had never before been offered to a woman. David felt the offer was a high honor and urged Nancy to accept it. He was confident he could find a job in his field in Washington. So, submitting to Nancy's career potential, they pulled up stakes and settled here.

"Some men would be threatened by this type of situation. If a man wanted to prove that he didn't need other people, if he were an emotional do-it-yourselfer, then he might resist the emergence of his wife's career, especially if it were an outstanding one. But David is a strong man, eager and able to become a servant to Nancy's development. That is healthy 'headship' and management."

This is how we know what love is: Jesus Christ laid down his life for us. And we ought to lay down our lives for our brothers.

— 1 John 3:16 NIV —

*Nothing beats love at first sight
except love with insight.*

IN *One Woman's Liberation,* Shirley Boone writes: "Talk about blind adoration! When Pat and I married, I was so much in love I didn't have any sense at all. Pat has said in interviews that we married fully aware of the serious adjustments we'd have to make and the financial crises we'd face, but he was speaking strictly for himself. As far as I was concerned, I wasn't aware of anything except that he was wonderful and that life without him would be miserable.

"I understood exactly how Mary, Queen of Scots, must have felt when she said of James Bothwell, her third husband, 'I'd follow him to the ends of the earth in my petticoat,' because that's how I felt about Pat. . . . If Pat had suggested it, I would have gone with him to Timbuktu without batting an eye. He was my life. To me, he was perfect, and that was the beginning of our troubles, because anyone placed on a pinnacle can go in only one direction—down."

Shirley and Pat Boone worked through their differences to create a strong and lasting marriage, but the beginning of their true success as a couple came when they each recognized this cardinal truth—nobody's perfect.

The beginning of wisdom is this: Get wisdom,
and whatever you get, get insight.
Proverbs 4:7 RSV

The measure of a man is not how great his faith is but how great his love is.

DURING the course of their twenty-four years of marriage, Tom accumulated a fortune in the natural gas business. But suddenly, he watched the fruit of his labors slip away to creditors. Things became so desperate at one point that in order to make their house payment, he had to sell his wife Tina's engagement ring. Finally, Tom was forced out of business altogether. He and Tina lost everything they had.

When things looked the worst, Tom began a promising job in another industry and slowly he began to come out of his slump. Later while out to dinner one evening, Tina saw in Tom signs of his old exuberance. He took his wife's hand in his own, placed a ring on her finger and said, "Tina, you are like this diamond—beautiful, exquisite, precious." Tina thought her heart would burst.

"But where did you get the money?" she asked.

"You haven't known it," Tom confessed, "but for two years I've been giving plasma once a week. I saved all the money I was paid and last week I sold my hunting gear. The only hunting I want to do from now on is hunt for ways to love you more. You *are* my life."

Greater love has no man than this,
that a man lay down his life for his friends.
John 15:13 RSV

*Before marriage the three little words are,
"I love you."
After marriage they are, "Let's eat out."*

AUSTRALIAN James H. Jauncey writes in *Talking With the Heart,* "I once married a Norwegian soldier to a Mexican girl. He could speak a little English, but no Spanish. She could speak neither English nor Norwegian.

"How they got together I'll never know. And what might happen in the future as far as communication was concerned, I could not even guess.

"But if they were in bad shape language-wise, they were in an infinitely better position than many couples I have known who had complete mastery of the English language.

"My odd bridal couple had successfully gotten over their message of love to each other and they seemed in remarkable rapport. Perhaps communication is easy in that stage, language or no language.

"Later on, the emotions die down and the hidden needs arise. Learning to talk about the needs is a difficult art, and not many learn it."

But he that is married careth for the things that are of the world, how he may please his wife.

1 Corinthians 7:33 KJV

The direction of your thought life can determine the course of your marriage.

AS Train 8017 made its way through Salerno, Italy, on March 2, 1944, there was no indication of impending disaster. The chugging train didn't collide with anything on that rain-soaked evening. It didn't derail or burn. But shortly after 1:00 a.m., the train loaded with 600 passengers lumbered into the Galleria delle Armi. When the two locomotives pulling the train were halfway through the tunnel, their drivewheels began to slip. The wheels lost traction and the train stopped. All else is speculation since both engineers died. Carbon monoxide snuffed out the lives of nearly 500 people.

As analysts surveyed the wreckage, they found that the leading locomotive was unbraked, its controls set in reverse. The second locomotive was also unbraked, but its throttle was positioned "full ahead." The two locomotives had pulled and pushed against each other, each engineer obviously having fatally different ideas about what to do! Some have speculated that no lives would have been lost if the engineers had been in agreement about which direction to go.

Today, make a decision with your spouse that you will both move your thought life in the direction of God—then stay close by the controls of your minds.

Keep thy heart with all diligence; for out of it are the issues of life.
∽ Proverbs 4:23 KJV ∽

A loving spouse can see the good in you even when you can't.

22

NATHANIEL came home heartbroken. How could he tell his dear wife that he had just been fired from his job at the customhouse? The last thing he wanted her to think was that he was a failure, yet he felt as if the word "failure" was embroidered across his chest.

However to his surprise, when he told his wife what had happened, she responded with joy. "Now you can write your book!" she said optimistically.

"And what shall we live on while I am writing it?" Nathaniel replied dejectedly.

His wife Sophia immediately went to a drawer and to his amazement, pulled out a substantial sum of money and handed it to him.

"Where did you get this?" he said, completely shocked.

"I have always known you were a man of genius," Sophia said. "I knew that someday you would write a masterpiece. Every week, out of the money you gave me for the housekeeping, I saved a little bit. Here is enough to last us for one whole year."

So Nathaniel Hawthorne, buoyed by his wife's confidence, turned his hand to writing *The Scarlet Letter.*

Be patient with each other, making allowance
for each other's faults because of your love.
Ephesians 4:2 TLB

*Forgiveness is giving love when
there is no reason to.*

WHEN God forgives, something decisive happens. When we forgive, again, something decisive happens. In *Healing Life's Hurts*, Matthew and Dennis Linn tell of an inner-healing workshop they observed. The men and women present were all once divorced and had remarried. They had come to the retreat hoping for healing of the anger and hostility they felt toward their former spouses. During the weekend sessions, the remarried couples were slowly and prayerfully led into ways in which they could grow from their past relationships and use what they learned to build new patterns of love and forgiveness in their current marriages.

After a year, the group reunited to discuss what had happened in the aftermath of the retreat. The Linns reported: "Out of the seven who forgave a former spouse after years of resentment, five found that their former spouses had suddenly made an effort to forgive and build a bridge toward them. One suddenly called a week after the workshop, another traveled two thousand miles to see his family, and another wrote his first letter in ten silent years."

Forgiveness frees us to both give and receive love. It is one of the most important things we must practice in marriage.

Blessed are the merciful, for they shall obtain mercy.
Matthew 5:7 NKJV

*An argument is the longest distance
between two points.*

26

IN *Letters to Karen,* a book written to his daughter by Author Charlie W. Shedd, he shares "Our Seven Official Rules for a Good, Clean Fight." They are:

1. Before we begin we must both agree that the time is right.
2. We will remember that our only aim is deeper understanding.
3. We will check our weapons often to be sure they're not deadly.
4. We will lower our voices one notch instead of raising them two.
5. We will never quarrel or reveal private matters in public.
6. We will discuss an armistice whenever either of us calls "halt."
7. When we have come to terms, we will put it away till we both agree it needs more discussing.

Says Shedd, "No small part of the zest in a good marriage comes from working through differences. Learning to zig and zag with the entanglements; studying each other's reactions under pressure; handling one another's emotions intelligently— all these offer a challenge that simply can't be beat for sheer fun and excitement."

We can experience that "sheer fun and excitement" when we learn to apply the above rules for a good, clean fight and apply ourselves to open, honest communication.

When angry, do not sin; do not ever let your wrath
(your exasperation, your fury or indignation)
last until the sun goes down.
Ephesians 4:26 AMP

It is our uniqueness that gives freshness and vitality to a relationship.

MARK and Joanne were not only married, but they shared a clinical practice as dentists. To the outsider, Mark and Joanne seemed like complete opposites, which they readily admitted they were.

"We're different in virtually every way," Joanne admits. "Mark can't balance a checkbook, but I'm good at accounting. He is great at dealing with the salesmen who come in to the clinic; I tend to buy too much of everything they show me. I'm much neater than he is, but he doesn't bring home problems the way I do. When we got out of dental school, we were advised *never* to go into partnership with each other."

"For awhile," Mark added, "we took that advice. Then I realized that I was bringing my books home for Joanne to balance and she was asking me to cancel orders from salesmen. So we decided that rather than deny our differences, we'd use them!"

Mark and Joanne sought a professional counselor who could advise them how to make their differences work for them rather than against them, but not promote their common weaknesses into codependency.

"We're unique," they conclude. "But we're also a team. If we were identical, we'd probably be bored."

For I am fearfully and wonderfully made.
Psalm 139:14 KJV

Men for the sake of getting a living forget to live.

COLUMNIST Erma Bombeck has written: "At some point in your life—if you are lucky—you throw practicality to the wind and start living.

"A lot of things can bring about your rebirth. With me, it was a case of the evening news. I was sitting around one night flipping between Dan, Peter, and Tom, who were giving me my state-of-the-world fix. After hearing about drugs, crime, bad air, tainted fish, holes in the atmosphere, cyanide-laced fruits, and people blowing each other up, I said aloud, 'That tears it. Life is too short to eat brown bananas.'

"I know that's a strange metaphor, but it sort of sums up my life. Every week, I buy fresh bananas, but I can't eat them until I've eaten up the semi-rotten ones from the week before. By the time they are gone, the fresh ones are getting rotten. . . .

"I took a long, hard look at my sensible life and began to question it. . . . This week I bought the prettiest bananas I could find. I'm in control. I'll eat them when I say they're ready to be eaten."

Don't get so caught up in the practice of life that you forget to enjoy one another's company.

So don't worry at all about having enough food and clothing. Why be like the heathen? For they take pride in all these things and are deeply concerned about them. But your heavenly Father already knows perfectly well that you need them.

Matthew 6:31-32 TLB

The best way to hold a man is in your arms.

OUR ability to become emotionally involved with others and to be vulnerable to them is directly related to our experiences of having been stroked, caressed, and cuddled as children. We learn affection from the tender models in our lives. We learn security from the warmth of being held close.

Before birth, a baby is enveloped in the soft, warm embrace of the womb. After birth, the child who is left untouched and uncuddled will form a bond with anything given it to touch, such as a stuffed toy. If all human tactile experience is denied, the baby will eventually die.

Our need for touch continues throughout our lifetime. In fact, our body chemistry actually changes when we are physically close to another person. When a person is touched, the amount of hemoglobin in the blood—which carries oxygen and helps prevent disease and speed recovery from illness—increases significantly. In one animal study, rabbits that were held close and stroked often developed less hardening of the arteries than unstroked, unhugged rabbits!

If you are uncomfortable with intimacy or close contact, you can learn to become comfortable. It will require effort, but the results will be worth it!

May your unfailing love be my comfort,
according to your promise to your servant.
Psalm 119:76 NIV

*The best way for you and your spouse
to guarantee some time without
the kids is to do the dinner dishes together.*

34

GROANING as he helped his wife wash the dishes one evening, the Reverend John Byrnell protested, "This isn't a man's job!"

His wife immediately wiped her hands and reached for the family Bible on the nearby dining table. "Oh, yes it is," she said as she turned to 2 Kings 21:13 KJV and read aloud to her husband, "I will wipe Jerusalem as a man wipeth a dish, wiping it, and turning it upside down."

Doing things together is the essence of a healthy marriage. You may not feel led to or be able to do what one married couple, both ordained Presbyterian ministers, did in Bellevue, Washington, but their example is certainly one of a shared life:

- They joined their names with a hyphen, each using the full hyphenated name.
- They shared one ministerial position, both as "associate pastor."
- Each was on the job half the time and each received half the pay.
- Each did half the household work.

Having time together won't just happen. You must purpose to make it happen. Write it in your calendar and treat it as if it were an appointment with a very important business associate or client—it is!

Two can accomplish more than twice as much as one,
for the results can be much better.

Ecclesiastes 4:9 TLB

What is a home without a Bible? 'Tis a home where daily bread for the body is provided, but the soul is never fed.

LEONARD E. LESOURD has written about his late wife, Catherine Marshall, the author of *Christy:* "Bibles were scattered throughout our house . . . all editions, plus reference books and concordances. We often went to bed, turned out the light, and listened to a chapter of scripture on tape. If she could have found a way to spread Bible passages on a slice of bread, Catherine would have devoured it.

"When upset or under spiritual assault or in physical pain, Catherine would go to her office, kneel by her chair, and open her Bible. . . . She would read, then pray, then read, then pray some more. She liked to pray with the Bible clutched in her hands. . . . She would rest her case on its promises. Catherine didn't read the Bible for solace or inspiration, but to have an encounter with the Lord. . . . I think these were the most intense moments of her life. Catherine's passion for the Word permeated her whole life. It undergirded her writing. It formed a base for us as a married team in the making of family decisions. It provided substance to her counseling of people through the mail. I'm convinced it was also the basis for her inner vitality, her charisma, and the mantle of authority she wore with some reluctance."

It is written, "Man shall not live by bread alone, but by every word that proceeds from the mouth of God."
— Matthew 4:4 NKJV

*The closer a man and his wife get to Christ,
the clearer they see how important it is
for them to stay close to each other.*

A CHILD once asked his father to draw a picture of a stepladder for him. The father did as he was asked. Then his son said, "No, Dad, you left out something." The father looked again at the double upside-down V he had drawn on the page and the lines he had drawn as the ladder's steps. "What did I leave out?" he asked. The little boy replied, "The part where you put the paint can."

The little boy may have been more interested in paint cans than a properly engineered ladder. But what the father later realized was that the "crosspiece" that extends to provide a resting place for paint cans is the one part of a stepladder that is truly indispensable! Without it, the inverted V shape of a ladder would collapse to the ground. It is the crosspiece that allows a stepladder to support weight.

If a couple is only joined by a recited vow, their marriage may quickly collapse. If Christ, however, forms the crosspiece that holds their lives into a sturdy triangular shape, they can withstand much pressure. With Christ in the center, a couple grows closer to each other as they grow closer to Christ.

And though a man might prevail against one who is alone, two will withstand him. A threefold cord is not quickly broken.

Ecclesiastes 4:12 RSV

Nothing is so strong as gentleness.
Nothing is so gentle as real strength.

IN *God Works the Night Shift*, Ron Mehl writes of Joe Knapp, who was as "fearless and aggressive as a bulldozer." He drove a beer truck down the Oregon highways and had a streak of mean that went clear to the bone. But Joe found the extended hand of God on a cold, snowy night in Portland, Oregon. Trying to navigate the snowy streets, his truck stalled in front of a church. He went in the church and was converted that night to Christ. Joe eventually went to the mission field and became the pastor of a large Protestant church. Joe was bombastic and tough, though his wife Virginia was a quiet, gracious woman.

What Mehl most remembered about Joe, however, was not his toughness; it was "his extraordinary tenderness shown his wife as she lay in a rest home. Joe knew she was afraid to be alone, so every day this dear man, who years earlier could have single-handedly tossed everyone out of a bar, would visit with his little wife long into the night. Every day as Joe sat at her side, he would tell her how much he loved her. . . . But most of all, he would hold her hand." Joe was strong enough to be gentle.

Thou hast also given me the shield of Thy salvation,
And Thy right hand upholds me;
And Thy gentleness makes me great.

Psalm 18:35

Love makes a house a home.

EVEN though he was single, at age thirty-two Bill decided it was time to buy a house. He found a modestly priced four-bedroom home and began to visualize how he could use the rooms. A few months later, however, he found himself engaged to marry a woman who had three young daughters. Two years after their marriage, Bill and his wife, Dee, had a baby. The gym and TV room he had envisioned in his new home never materialized!

It took Bill and Dee four jobs to pay for the life they had chosen, but although their schedules were relentless, Bill couldn't help but conclude, "Ain't life grand?" Eventually, his stepdaughters began to leave home and Bill once again made plans for the spare rooms in the house. But his elderly parents needed help, and Bill and Dee invited them to move in. Even in getting up at night to help his ailing father, Bill still was of the opinion, "Ain't life grand?"

After more than twenty-five years, Bill still doesn't have his "dream house." What he has had, however, is two decades of a real *home*.

Any living space that's filled with selfless caring can be called a home.

You will be happy and it will be well with you.
Your wife shall be like a fruitful vine, within your house,
your children like olive plants around your table.
Psalm 128:2-3

You will never "find" time for anything.
If you want time, you must make it.

COLLEEN EVANS writes in *My Lover, My Friend:* "I'm not sure exactly what I said, but between sniffs and sobs . . . I told him how hungry I was to be with him, to have time to talk and dream, alone. . . .

"We sat and talked for a very long time, saying things we both wanted and needed to hear. . . . I remember Louie thanked me for being honest about my feelings. . . . And then he did a simple, practical—and, to me, very beautiful—thing. He took his little date book from his pocket, and looked until he found a free night. It happened to be Thursday of the following week, and he said, 'That's our night'. . . . Out of that night came a decision to put aside time every week for the same purpose . . . and so it has been in all the years since . . . Thursday night.

"Now I'm sure many couples are able to find time for each other in an easy, unscheduled way, and that's wonderful. But that didn't work for us. With our kind of life we found we had to *make* time."

Whatever your hand finds to do, do it with all your might.
Ecclesiastes 9:10 NIV

The kind of music people should have in their homes is domestic harmony.

TWO men once made small talk at a party: "You and your wife seem to get along very well," one man said. "Don't you ever have differences?"

"Sure," said the other. "We often have differences, but we get over them quickly."

"How do you do that?" the first man asked.

"Simple," said the second. "I don't tell her we have them."

In *Letters to Philip*, Charles Shedd describes a slightly different situation—harmony that comes after love has conquered conflict. He writes: "In one town where I lived two rivers met. There was a bluff high above them where you could sit and watch their coming together. . . . Those two nice streams came at each other like fury. I have actually seen them on days when it was almost frightening to watch. They clashed in a wild commotion of frenzy and confusion. . . . Then, as you watched, you could almost see the angry white caps pair off, bow in respect to each other, and join forces as if to say, 'Let us get along now. Ahead of us there is something better.' Sure enough, on downstream, at some distance, the river swept steadily on once more."

And above all these put on love, which binds everything together in perfect harmony.

Colossians 3:14 RSV

Marriage must exemplify friendship's highest ideal, or else it will be a failure.

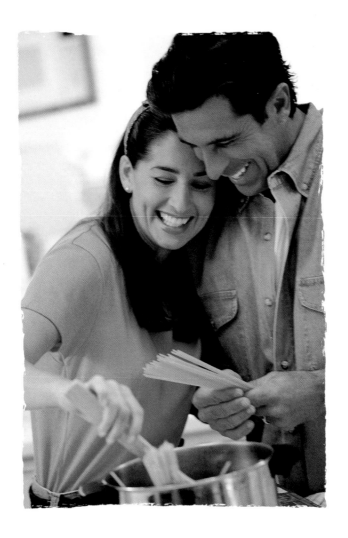

ALTHOUGH Kim wasn't a great cook, she decided to try to make something "from scratch" for the church potluck. On the way to the event, both she and her husband Hank could smell the charred aroma of scorched sauce.

When they arrived at the potluck, Kim's casserole was placed on the table along with the other food dishes. Before anyone came to the table, Kim spooned a bit of the casserole out for Hank to taste it. The look on his face confirmed her worst nightmare.

Before anyone else came to the table, Hank picked up Kim's casserole and announced to the group that he was going to make a pig out of himself and eat Kim's casserole all by himself. He noted that there were plenty of other hot dishes, salads, and desserts for the rest of them—but after all, he asked, how often did he get his favorite dish?

Hank sat in a corner courageously eating most of the "casserole for four" before anyone else could taste it. And though they laughed about it later, Kim told her friends for years, "I knew then I had married a man I would do my best to keep forever."

And here is how to measure it—the greatest love is shown when a person lays down his life for his friends.
John 15:13 TLB

A wise lover values not so much the gift of the lover as the love of the giver.

THE ability to give is, in itself, a gift—a manifestation of God's goodness to a person. If you have trouble giving, ask God to give you a spirit of generosity and a willingness to give!

George MacDonald writes in *The Word of Jesus on Prayer,* "For the real good of every gift it is essential, first that the giver be in the gift—as God always is, for He is love—and next, that the receiver know and receive the giver in the gift. Every gift of God is but a harbinger of His greatest and only sufficing gift— that of Himself. No gift unrecognized as coming from God is at its own best: therefore many things that God would gladly give us must wait until we ask for them, that we may know whence they come. When in all gifts we find Him, then in Him we shall find all things."

There is no relationship where this kind of gift giving is more important and more life-enhancing than in the marriage relationship. You know your spouse better than anyone, and your spouse knows you. When you give your spouse a gift of your love, you're giving more of yourself.

How fair is thy love, my sister, my spouse! . . .
and the smell of thine ointments than all spices!
Song of Solomon 4:10 KJV

There is no more lovely, friendly, and charming relationship, communion, or company than a good marriage.

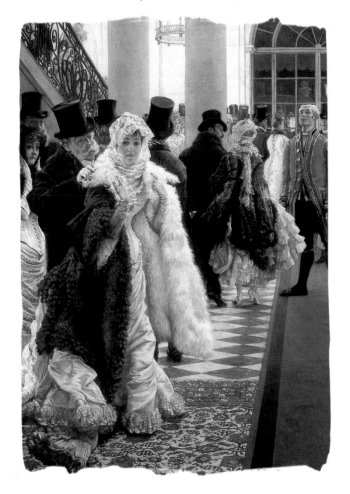

ELIZABETH endured hell on earth during her formative years. She was one of eleven children born to a father who was an oppressive, dictatorial tyrant. His angry rages often sent sensitive Elizabeth to her bed with any variety of ills.

It wasn't until she was forty years old that Elizabeth met Robert. Robert did not see her as a sickly middle-aged invalid. Rather, he saw her as a beautiful, talented woman just waiting to blossom. He loved her with all his heart and withstood several brutal confrontations with Elizabeth's controlling father before he finally won her hand in marriage.

Glowing in love for each other, they traveled the European continent, marveling at God's wonders and at their own love. At forty-three, Elizabeth gave birth to a healthy baby. Their lives were full and beautiful. In great joy, Elizabeth wrote to her husband the incomparable words of "How Do I Love Thee?" True loveliness and charm had wonderfully entered Elizabeth Barrett's life when she became Elizabeth Barrett Browning.

When we pour the balm of love on our spouse we can help bring healing to past hurts and encourage them to walk in God's wonderful plan for their life.

A wife of noble character is her husband's crown.
 Proverbs 12:4 NIV

No marriage is all sunshine, but two people can share one umbrella if they huddle close.

THE Blue Nile is a rushing, churning river, which gains its energy from the mountains down which it descends. It carries with it much of the rich and muddy soil from the country through which it passes to the Nile delta far away.

In the delta, the Blue Nile is joined by the White Nile, a sleepy, peaceful river which flows across the plains. As their names indicate, the White Nile is a clear river in comparison to the Blue.

Once they join together into the same riverbed, these two rivers maintain their distinct qualities and colors for many, many miles. From high above, one can clearly see the muddy currents of the Blue Nile, and the clear waters of the White. They are separate, yet united. The longer the rivers share the same riverbed, however, the more their currents intermingle, until the two rivers truly become one powerful and life-giving waterway.

When tough times hit a marriage or disagreements erupt, make a decision that you will pull together, rather than allow yourself to be pulled apart by temporary circumstances, momentary conflicts, or resolvable differences. Choose to flow together. The longer you do, the more "one" you will become.

If two lie down together, then they have warmth;
but how can one be warm alone?
Ecclesiastes 4:11 AMP

My most brilliant achievement was to be able to persuade my wife to marry me.

SHORTLY after Bill and Gail were married, they saw a theater production. Gail thought the leading man was extremely attractive, but Bill disagreed. "It wasn't his physical appearance," Gail said. "He was kind and sensitive, strong in an inner way. That's what I find attractive in a man. Though you don't always act that way, I know you are strong and self-confident on the inside. I love you for that."

Bill was stunned. He saw himself as anything but self-confident and strong. Usually he let others have their way—to the point where he even let others push him around. So he said, "I thought about what Gail said and decided, I *do* have those qualities and I ought to show them." The next day Bill had a confrontation at work. Although he was nervous, he stood his ground. And with Gail cheering him on, he was soon demonstrating his quiet strength at home and in the community, too.

Years later, Bill said, "Gail saw something in me that I hadn't seen in myself. I became someone I never would have become without her support and encouragement."

Today, purpose to encourage your spouse. Shower him or her with praise and love.

To every thing there is a season. . . . A time to get.
∾ Ecclesiastes 3:1,6 KJV ∾

The bonds of matrimony are worthless
unless the interest is kept up.

58

A MAGNET has two poles. If it doesn't, it isn't a magnet! It's only a useless hunk of scrap iron. One of the greatest danger signals in a marriage is when either partner no longer feels attracted to the other. This attraction actually has very little to do with youth or sex appeal as some might think. Attraction is based on how we define and perceive "beauty"—which is an inner quality, not merely a cosmetic or superficial state of prettiness or style. True beauty lies in the image of God. When we see another person as being created in God's image, we begin to see more and more facets of their being and appreciate more and more of their beauty. The more we acknowledge the beauty of their creation, the more we are attracted to their beauty.

Part of keeping the magnet working is seeing your spouse as "God's creation in process." Your spouse may be *influenced* and *encouraged* by you, but ultimately your spouse is God's creation. Your spouse's beauty is rooted in what God is doing in his or her life.

You are privileged to watch your spouse's beauty unfold and to enjoy the person your spouse is becoming!

Live happily with the woman you love through
the fleeting days of life, for the wife God gives you is
your best reward down here for all your earthly toil.
Ecclesiastes 9:9 TLB

Marriage may be inspired by music, soft words, and perfume; but its security is manifest in work, consideration, respect, and well-fried bacon.

ONE might not think of a bank's monthly newsletter as the place to read about the importance of good manners in marriage, but consider these wise words a staff member at the Royal Bank of Canada once wrote:

"Many of the things that disturb family life are the product of original mistakes compounded by bad manners. Walter Hines Page, distinguished United States ambassador to Great Britain, said: 'The more I find out about diplomatic customs, and the more I hear of the little-big troubles of others, the more need I find to be careful about details of courtesy.'

"If love is the foundation of happy marriage, good manners are the walls and diplomacy is the roof.

"Manners for two are fixed by the same rules as are manners for the million, based upon the Golden Rule. They spring from kindness, courtesy, and consideration, with a dash of *savoir faire*—the faculty of knowing just what to do and how to do it."

For some, the secret of a happy marriage lies in finding out what pleases the other person, then doing those things. For others, the secret lies in discovering what irritates, annoys, or angers another person, then not doing those things!

Nevertheless let each one of you in particular so love his own wife as himself, and let the wife see that she respects her husband.

Ephesians 5:33 NKJV

*A successful marriage requires falling in love
many times, always with the same person.*

A MAN who had been married to his childhood sweetheart for more than thirty years, said, "I still like to hold my wife's hand." He went on to admit, however, that he enjoyed holding his wife's hand for a different reason now than he had when he was a teenager.

"When we were kids," he reflected, "I got an electric spark when I touched her hand. Now when my life seems filled with too much electricity, I get a sense of peace when I hold her hand."

The touch of a hand can mean more than, "I love you." Sometimes it can mean, "I care," or, "I need you," or simply, "I'm here."

The roots of love become branched and intertwined over time. Love and intimacy are found in many aspects of marriage. Sometimes those are rooted in compassion, sometimes in a sense of doing what is right. Sometimes they grow from giving help, other times from receiving help.

Take a fresh look at your spouse today. Change your perspective. Find something new to appreciate. You may very well find yourself falling in love all over again!

I will betroth you to me forever; I will betroth you in righteousness and justice, in love and compassion.

*The great thing about being married
a long time is falling in love with the same
person again . . . and again . . . and again.*

ANN and Paul were intelligent, attractive, warm human beings. Married twenty years, they had four children. On the surface, their lives appeared successful. But inside, things were sour. They both worked at demanding jobs and had little time for each other. As communication faltered, they began to confide in friends, who soon became more serious interests. As the couple considered divorce, they sought out a Christian counselor in the hopes that he might help them make the painful journey of rediscovering each other.

The counselor encouraged each of them to take their hurts to the Lord, the only One Who could truly forgive them and heal them, and to pray together. Prayer was a risk for them. What if it didn't work? Still, they were willing to try. Over time, they discovered the more they prayed alone and together, the softer their hearts grew. A new love was born, and their minister led them in a reuniting service. With their children present, they rededicated their lives to Christ and to each other . . . there wasn't a dry eye in the house.

Not every couple may need such a service, but every marriage needs reuniting in some way every day.

Let thy fountain be blessed: and rejoice with the wife of thy youth . . . and be thou ravished always with her love.
Proverbs 5:18-19 KJV

*To keep your marriage brimming with love
in the loving cup, whenever you're wrong,
admit it, whenever you're right, shut up.*

MARIE LOUISE DE LA RAMEE says in *Ouida,* "There are many moments in friendship, as in love, when silence is beyond words. The faults of our friend may be clear to us, but it is well to seem to shut our eyes to them.

"Friendship is usually treated by the majority of mankind as a tough and everlasting thing which will survive all manner of bad treatment. But this is an exceedingly great and foolish error: It may die in an hour of a single unwise word."

If "I love you" is the most important three-word phrase in a marriage, "I'm sorry" is probably the most important two-word phrase! The more a spouse is willing to admit fault, the greater the likelihood the other spouse will also grow to be vulnerable enough to admit error. This is not to say that a person should apologize for an error that has not been made; to do so would be to become a doormat or to manifest a false humility. When one is standing in the right, although the other cannot see it, the better approach is the no-word statement of silence. Not a "I know I'm right" silence, but a prayerful silence.

67

Confess to one another therefore your faults . . . and pray [also] for one another, that you may be healed and restored.
James 5:16 AMP

A marriage may be made in heaven, but the maintenance must be done on earth.

IN *Rock-Solid Marriage*, Robert and Rosemary Barnes write: "Last summer we went with a close friend to his ranch in Jackson Hole, Wyoming. At our friend Gary's insistence, we spent one whole day climbing the side of a mountain to get to see something he wanted us to see. We were both just exhausted and it got to the point that we really didn't care what was in that special valley. It couldn't be worth all that pain we were going through. He just kept insisting. 'Trust me,' he kept saying, 'you'll be glad you did this when we get there.'

"Three hours later, when our feet were blistered and we were dying of thirst, we finally reached our destination. Lying down on a side of a mountain, we were looking at the most beautiful valley and lake I had ever seen. The climb was long and it was agony, but it was more than worth it. Gary was right.

"In the beginning, God established marriage. It wasn't meant to be easy; nothing worth having is. It was meant to be fulfilling and completing. It takes work. But it's almost as if God is saying, 'Trust Me, it's worth the effort!'"

Practice what you have learned and received and heard and seen in me, and model your way of living on it, and the God of peace (of untroubled, undisturbed well-being) will be with you.

❧ Philippians 4:9 AMP ❧

The most impressive example of tolerance is a golden wedding anniversary.

70

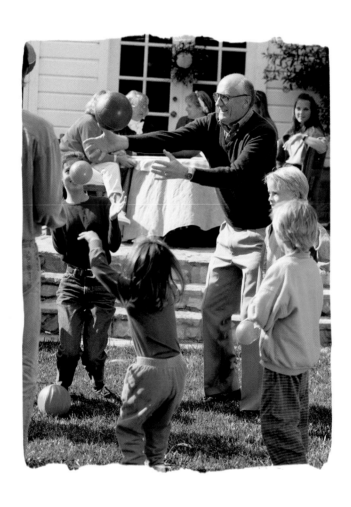

VIRGINIA sat silently as her husband of forty years, Frank, launched into a round of silly camp songs with the children and teens in their living room. The kids loved his enthusiastic singing, and he soon had them singing in rounds and tramping around the room while the adults made their way into quieter rooms.

One of Virginia's friends noticed that Virginia moved to freshen the buffet table as the songfest became more rowdy, then watched her retreat into the kitchen. The friend followed her and said, "Isn't Frank fun? What a sense of humor!" Virginia just smiled and said, "Actually, I hate those songs, and it bothers me when my otherwise very dignified husband acts so silly." Then she quickly added, "But, I've never told Frank that and I never will. He's having a good time, and that's what parties are all about. For that matter, I suspect he doesn't like my fussing so much about the food during a party, but he's never told me so. I guess you could say we give each other enough space to be ourselves."

Tolerance means letting another person live uncriticized as they manifest all of their human foibles and quirks.

Let your fountain [of human life] be blessed [with the rewards of fidelity], and rejoice in the wife of your youth.

Proverbs 5:18 AMP

Lay aside life-harming heaviness and entertain a cheerful disposition.

IN *The Mystery of Marriage*, Mike Mason writes about a day in which he and his wife watched a pair of hawks: "As they drew closer to us they began to descend in great lazy swoops down the blue invisible banisters of the air. . . . I parked the car, and we got out to watch. The sunlight spilled soft auras around their splayed forms. We could see frayed feathers, translucent at the tips. Not once did either bird move a wing muscle. They held themselves perfectly steady, taut yet relaxed, angling against the air and gliding . . . turning in slow and beautiful spirals that meshed together and then away . . . like a pair of ice skaters.

"The longer we watched, the clearer it became that these hawks were doing absolutely nothing of any practical import. They were simply playing. They were enjoying the warm blueness of the day, the strength and skill in their wings, the fun of flying . . . there was something in this soaring dance of the pair of them, with a whole sky all to themselves, which spoke directly to me, not just of play and freedom on a summer's day, but of the shining beauty of love, the pure ease and joy of companionship."

A glad heart makes a cheerful countenance,
but by sorrow of heart the spirit is broken.
Proverbs 15:13 AMP

How to be a happily married couple can never really be taught, only learned.

A MAN and wife were celebrating their golden wedding anniversary. After spending most of the day with relatives and friends at a party given in their honor, they returned home tired, but a little hungry. They decided to have a little snack of tea and bread and butter before retiring. While the wife began making the tea the husband opened a new loaf of bread, took out the end piece, buttered it, and handed it to his wife. He was not prepared for her reaction.

"For fifty years you have been dumping the heel on me," she exploded. "I won't take this lack of concern any longer. I'm fed up with eating heels!" Her husband stared at her in shocked dismay, then finally spoke in a small, meek voice, "But the heel on the loaf is my favorite piece."

Sometimes it takes a lifetime to learn what a spouse truly likes and dislikes. It sometimes takes that long for a person to decide what they *personally* want out of life, and just exactly how they want to live. Be patient with your spouse as you "learn" all the lessons he or she embodies. And ask them if they like the heel!

And try to learn [in your experience] what is pleasing to the Lord [let your lives be constant proofs of what is most acceptable to Him].

Ephesians 5:10 AMP

What greater thing is there for two human souls than to feel that they are joined for life?

RAY ROSA grew up in Italy and came to the United States as a young man in 1921. He met and married his wife, Isabel, and they settled in Swampscott, Massachusetts, where Ray worked as a barber most of his life. After many years had gone by, Isabel became ill and was moved to a nursing home in a nearby town.

Ray's routine dramatically changed. Seven mornings a week, he would take the 10:25 bus to the nursing home, where he would stay until 5:30 in the evening. Isabel would be waiting for him in a wheelchair each morning. They would spend the day together, Ray helping Isabel with her needs and occasionally bringing his mandolin and singing Italian songs for the other patients at the home. He would usually give a haircut or two to some of the male patients and entertain them with barbershop stories. To those in the nursing home, Ray was a hero, the brightest part of any day, a source of warmth and laughter and encouragement.

Ray said he was simply fulfilling a promise he made years ago, a commitment to love forever "in sickness and in health."

What therefore God hath joined together, let no man put asunder.

Matthew 19:6 KJV

If we must disagree, let's disagree without being disagreeable.

78

THE lyrics of a song proclaim, "I am a rock, I am an island. And a rock feels no pain, and an island never cries." Unfortunately, those who live with rocks and islands often *do* feel pain and often cry.

People who think of themselves as being entirely self-sufficient are, in fact, selfish. They nearly always proclaim their opinions as the only ones that count, their feelings as the only ones that matter. Such a person is rarely capable of a good argument—they simply make speeches and walk away. If you are the spouse of such a person, Dr. James Dobson offers this advice: "Change that which can be altered, explain that which can be understood, teach that which can be learned, revise that which can be improved, resolve that which can be settled, and negotiate that which is open to compromise . . . accept that which cannot be changed."

If you and your spouse cannot find an area of agreement, accept the fact that you *disagree*. Rather than suffer in silence at another's selfish tirades, simply say, "I have another point of view." Openly acknowledging your disagreement may very well be your first point of agreement!

As far as it depends on you, live at peace with everyone.
Romans 12:18 AMP

Marriage is a marathon, not a sprint.

PSYCHOLOGISTS use the phrase "progressive menaces" in their professional vocabulary. This may not seem an ideal way to describe matrimony, but it does convey the idea that marriage is not static. It is ever changing. As with any normal relationship, a couple continually faces changing situations that require of each person a new orientation, a new pattern of reaction, a new way of facing life.

In individual lives, our greatest years of productivity usually come later in life. Wayne Dennis at Brooklyn College studied the lives of 156 well-known scientists who lived beyond the age of seventy. He found that the decades of the forties and fifties were their most productive. The years of sixties and seventies, while not as productive as the forties and fifties, were years of high output. But their twenties were their least productive years.

Four major poets who lived beyond eighty did more work in their last decade than they did between twenty and thirty. Tennyson was eighty when he wrote "Crossing the Bar." Michelangelo painted *The Last Judgment* at age sixty-six.

The most satisfying and fulfilling years of marriage are also likely to be later in life. Make your marriage one for the "long haul."

And Jacob served seven years for Rachel; and they seemed unto him but a few days, for the love he had to her.
— Genesis 29:20 KJV

$\mathcal{S}$haring the housework makes it
easier to share the love.

JOANNE KAUFMAN says that her best friend, Beth, has little appreciation for the game of golf. To her, it's a boring game that takes too long to play. "Nonetheless," Joanne writes, "every weekend, three seasons out of four, she's a fixture on a certain nine-hole course near her home in upstate New York. Why? The look of sheer delight in the eyes of her husband, Jerry, when she tees off.

"'Another reason is that he would be spending those five hours without me, and I like his company,' she says. And ultimately, lugging around a golf bag seems a small price to pay for the fact that Jerry does all the laundry—including the ironing.

"'And,' adds Beth with a smile, 'there have been other benefits.' On a recent vacation to Florida, after eighteen holes of golf in a gale force wind, her husband didn't squawk a whit about going on a major shopping expedition."

Sometimes in order to get your spouse to do what you enjoy doing, you need to do what your spouse enjoys. In the end, doing both "his and her" activities means double the amount of time spent together, rather than each person going their own way.

Bear one another's burdens, and so fulfil the law of Christ.
☙ Galatians 6:2 RSV ❧

Don't take yourself too seriously, and never fail to take your spouse seriously enough.

84

BILL and Lynne Hybels write in *Fit to Be Tied:* "Picture this: It is midnight. The full moon is postcard perfect and the breeze is warm. Lynne and I are sitting on a park bench at a wooded camp in Wisconsin. Twenty years old. Dating seriously. No one around . . . I wrap my arms around her. This is what it's all about, I think. Lynne lifts her head and looks deeply into my eyes. 'Bill, I just don't feel close to you right now.' . . . 'For heaven's sake, honey, what do you want?' I hug her a little tighter, laugh off her comment, and dismiss it from my mind.

"Big mistake! If I could play that scene over, I would do it this way. I would take her hands off my shoulders, slide about a foot away, look her straight in the eye and say, 'Why don't you feel close to me? . . . If you don't know exactly why you said it, just start talking about how you feel. Maybe we can figure it out.'

"A response like that would have set a precedent for honest communication that could have made our marriage much easier."

Do nothing from selfishness or empty conceit, but with humility of mind let each of you regard one another as more important than himself.

Philippians 2:3

Good listeners make good lovers.

"ONE year after our wedding, Rosemary and I decided to spend part of the summer in Europe," writes Robert Barnes in *Rock-Solid Marriage.* "It was far from a luxury trip, as we traveled on the European rail system and stayed in hotels. One of Rosemary's dreams was to see the great art museums of Europe. One museum was enough for me. . . .

"It was surprising to me how much time she could spend standing in front of those paintings. They didn't mean anything to me. The difference was that she had spent part of her life being taught about the great artists of the world.

"Toward the end of our stay in Europe I too was able to enjoy these museums because I let her teach me about what we were looking at. Until then, we were looking at the same works of art but seeing different things.

"There's no doubt about it. Individuals enter into marriage speaking different languages. They experience things differently. They talk and listen differently. And they love and grow their self-esteem differently. Marriage can be tough unless the couple is willing to set aside some time to learn from each other."

Listen to advice and accept instruction,
and in the end you will be wise.
Proverbs 19:20 NIV

*It takes two
to make a quarrel.*

WALTER Trobisch once said, "When a couple comes to me and wants to get married, I always ask them if they have once had a real quarrel—not just a casual difference of opinion—but a real fight.

"Many times they will say: 'Oh no! Pastor, we love each other.'

"Then I tell them: 'Quarrel first—and then I will marry you.'

"The point is, of course, not the quarreling, but the ability to be reconciled to each other. This ability must be trained and tested before marriage. Not sex, but rather this quarrel test, is, as I see it, a 'required' premarital experience.

"The question is, therefore: Are we able to forgive each other and to give in to each other?"

Harsh words and arguments often involve an eruption of long-harbored bitterness. We may not be able to control all the factors that lead to hurt feelings, but we each can keep bitterness from growing in our hearts. If an issue warrants discussion, discuss it the very day the issue arises. If you don't act upon a hurt by the day's end, consider the issue past. Burn the bridges of that hurt and don't look back on it.

A soft answer turns away wrath,
But a harsh word stirs up anger.

Proverbs 15:1 NKJV

Love is the one business in which it pays to be an absolute spendthrift: Give it away; splash it over; empty your pockets shake the basket; and tomorrow you'll have more than ever.

LOVE is often called the "queen" of the fruit of the Spirit, the supreme manifestation of the Christian character. Donald Grey Barnhouse has made this very clear in his description of the fruit of the Spirit (see Galatians 5:22, 23):

> Love is the key.
> Joy is love singing.
> Peace is love resting.
> Longsuffering is love enduring.
> Kindness is love's touch.
> Goodness is love's character.
> Faithfulness is love's habit.
> Gentleness is love's self-forgetfulness.
> Self-control is love holding the reins.

A strong marriage is founded upon love. Sustaining that love is an ongoing privilege. Begin and end each day with words of love and acts of kindness for each other. Pour your love out upon one another; don't withhold it in anger or resentment. Let your love spill over into joy. Let love fill your home with peace. Endure irritations and difficulties with kindness and goodness. Be faithful to your spouse in word and deed. Love gently, controlling anger or displeasure.

Don't be like the man who responded to his wife when she complained that he never told her he loved her: "I told you I loved you on our wedding day, and if I ever change my mind, I'll let you know." Share your expressions of love generously and frequently!

Give, and it will be given to you. A good measure, pressed down, shaken together and running over, will be poured into your lap. For with the measure you use, it will be measured to you.

Luke 6:38 NIV

Love is friendship set on fire.

COLLEEN and Louie Evans write in *My Lover, My Friend*, "Ken and Hilda were in their early sixties when we were in our twenties—and naturally we felt that sex was invented for people of our age. How wrong we were! One day Hilda took me aside and said, 'Oh, Coke, since Ken has retired, we're having so much fun! We have time to do things we've wanted to do for years. And our sex life!—well, it's never been so good!' I gave Hilda a great big hug because I felt so happy for her—and for me, because she had expanded my limited idea of what happens to sex in the later years.

"Ken and Hilda are in their eighties now, and the miles separate us from them. But the picture and message on their Christmas card each year assure us that life is still very capable of producing a large twinkle in their eyes!"

Many young people enter marriage with what one man once described as "flaming hormones." But what those who have been married several decades often know is that physical love grows even sweeter and more satisfying as one's friendship in marriage deepens and expands.

Many waters cannot quench love, neither can floods drown it.

⤴ Song of Solomon 8:7 RSV ⤵

Best friends make the best spouses.

IS your spouse your best friend? How privileged you are if the answer is "yes." Perhaps an even more important question to ask is this: "Are you a good friend to your spouse?" In being a good friend, you very often gain a best friend!

A true friend is someone to whom you can empty your heart—a heart often made to feel "full" by many different sources of passion, concern, or worry.

Francis Bacon once wrote: "We know diseases of stoppings and suffocations are the most dangerous in the body; and it is not much otherwise in the mind: you may take sarza to open the liver, steel to open the spleen, flower of sulphur for the lungs, castoreum for the brain; but no receipt openeth the heart but a true friend, to whom you may impart griefs, joys, fears, hopes, suspicions, counsels, and whatsoever lieth upon the heart to oppress it, in a kind of civil shrift or confusion."

One of the best gifts you can give your spouse and your children is listening ears. Be a friend of the four C's: compassion, caring, consideration, and comfort. Those four traits never grow old or fall out of fashion.

There is a friend that sticketh closer than a brother.

Proverbs 18:24 KJV

Love is a product of habit.

THE traditional marriage vows recited by most couples include the phrases, "in sickness and in health," "for richer or poorer," and "for better or worse." There's a reason! Even the best relationships include times that qualify as sick, poor, and worse.

A young woman once phoned her mother and cried, "Mother, I had no idea marriage meant washing and ironing so many shirts!" Her mother wisely counseled, "Think of each shirt you iron as an act of love." The young woman took her mother's advice and just below the neckline on each collar she ironed, she planted a big kiss, complete with a tint of lipstick.

A marriage may involve washing and drying millions of dishes and making millions of beds and paying thousands of bills and scrubbing the floor thousands of times. It will mean emptying the trash and mowing the lawn thousands of times, and raking perhaps billions of leaves. But if you make each mundane chore related to your marriage an act of love, you'll find your feelings for your spouse growing sweeter, not bitterer.

Love in a marriage means doing many things you don't like. But it brings rewards you can reap in no other relationship!

Little children, let us not love in word or speech
but in deed and in truth.
I John 3:18 RSV

*Love's lasting comes in erasing
the boundary line between
"mine" and "yours."*

"THERE is something amphibious about marriage, something neither fish nor fowl," writes Mike Mason in *The Mystery of Marriage*. "It is like a three-legged sack race or a cloth-covered dancing horse, except that it is not only the feet and body but one's whole being that gets tangled up in the other person's. Marriage is not just a sharing but a mingling of identities, a consanguinity of psyches. It is a blend so intimate that it actually becomes hard to tell where one person leaves off and the other begins. People will peer and peer, for example, at a couple's offspring, trying to determine which one of the parents they resemble. Perhaps in a mysterious way what they are really trying to do is to tell the couple themselves apart, to separate again what has become impossibly intertwined. Not that this uncanny congruousness of the flesh of inner lives is always a very obvious or noticeable fact; but it becomes conspicuous in the birth of a child or at other times of crisis or exposure, at times when the hidden realities of lives float suddenly and dramatically to the surface."

That is truly what it means to become "one flesh."

But that as a matter of equality your abundance at the present time should supply their want, so that their abundance may supply your want, that there may be equality.
∾ 2 Corinthians 8:14 RSV ∾

Love must be learned, and learned again and again; there is no end to it.

CONSTANT arguing over Fred's thoughtlessness plagued the marriage of Sarah and Fred. From his perspective, he was simply very busy in his computer-programming business, a task that took all his concentration. Sarah was fed up with his forgetting her birthday and their anniversary. "Finally," she said, "I decided that fighting with him just made things worse. So I sat down and asked myself, *What other course could I take?*" She remembered how pleased Fred had been when she hugged and kissed him each time he brought her the slightest trinket. So she waited for a chance to praise him again in that way.

A few days later, Fred brought home a book she'd asked him to bring from the library. Sarah thanked him as if he had given her a diamond. "He looked at me as if I'd gone nuts," she said, "but I could tell that he knew I was pleased. After a while, I noticed that Fred actually started looking for ways to give and pay attention to me because he enjoyed being appreciated. I didn't care what his motivation was, I enjoyed his company and the creative things he was doing for me."

*And this I pray, that your love may abound yet
more and more in knowledge and in all judgment.*
Philippians 1:9 KJV

Matrimony—the high sea for which
no compass has yet been invented.

THERE'S no such thing as being able to put a marriage on "automatic pilot." You may be able to preset all the dials on your microwave oven, or preset your coffee pot to have coffee ready when you wake up, but you can't preset a relationship.

Neither is a marriage some type of rapid transit system with predictable stops along the way. Each marriage moves in its own direction, and develops at its own pace, having its own set of obstacles.

A marriage involves a commitment, not a contract. A contract can be instantly completed, signed, sealed, and delivered. A commitment, on the other hand, is a lifetime adventure. It may begin within a few minutes, but you can never arrive at a full-blown, fully satisfying marriage quickly.

Keep in mind as you sail the high seas of your marriage that:

When you hit storm-swept seas, you may have to work a little harder, but there's always peace after the storm.

If more than one hand is on the rudder, they need to be moving in the same direction.

Sometimes the safest thing to do is to lower the sails and let the wind take you where it will.

There are three things too wonderful for me to understand—
no, four! . . . How a ship finds its way across the heaving ocean.
The growth of love between a man and a girl.
Proverbs 30:18 TLB

Marriage is not for wimps.

EDITH SCHAEFFER tells of a time when her husband, Francis, visited a couple only to find the husband packing to leave in the morning. He intended to run away with a girl from his workplace with whom he was infatuated. Francis spent the entire night talking to the man, even though he wasn't particularly welcome. He pointed out the many causes for their troubles and said, "Let Edith talk to your wife, then you go and *give up your job,* and go away for a three-week honeymoon."

The next day, Edith spent several hours talking to his wife while she did her chores. She discovered the young woman had a stiff Mid-Victorian upbringing. So Edith advised her "to get an exotic black nightgown, some sexy underwear, some very different types of daytime clothes, have her hair done in a completely new style, buy a new kind of perfume, and go off on this planned second honeymoon determined to really forgive her husband." The two took their trip, putting each other before their material lives and staid upbringing, and they made a most amazing discovery of each other over the next three weeks.

They are grandparents today, with a beautiful family!

Let marriage be held in honor (esteemed worthy, precious, of great price and especially dear) in all things. And thus let the marriage bed be undefiled . . . for God will judge.

Hebrews 13:4 AMP

A joyful marriage is a bit of heaven on earth.

HOME has been called "heaven's fallen sister." Our homes can't help but bear at least a partial imprint of our fallen world. And yet, home holds the greatest potential for being like heaven of any place on earth. A godly home, built upon heaven's principles, can be the sweetest place to be!

When we think of our earthly homes as being a reflection of the heavenly home of our Father, we must ask ourselves, *What must God's home be like?*

Surely it is a place where there are no harsh words, no prolonged silences born of anger. It must be a place where each person is made to feel special, important, and valued beyond measure. It is a place of laughter and gladness, a place each person would desire to return to at the end of a difficult day. It must be a place of nourishment and growth, a place of total acceptance and unconditional love. Every person in God's home would surely be willing to share his or her innermost secrets, dreams, and hopes.

The good news is that we have the privilege of creating our homes to mirror heaven. It is within our power—with God's help—to do so!

Enjoy life with the woman whom you love all the days of your fleeting life which He has given to you under the sun; for this is your reward in life.

Ecclesiastes 9:9

A happy marriage is a long conversation which always seems too short.

ANNE MORROW was a delicate person—not dull or incompetent, just a quiet, timid woman. Her father was ambassador to Mexico when she met a young pilot who was visiting south of the border for the U.S. State Department. He had just won a $40,000 prize for being the first pilot to fly across the Atlantic. They fell deeply in love.

Anne could easily have been eclipsed by her husband's shadow. But she wrote: "To be deeply in love is, of course, a great liberating force and the most common experience that frees. . . . Ideally, both members of a couple in love free each other to new and different worlds. I was no exception to the general rule. The sheer fact of finding myself loved was unbelievable and changed my world. The man I was to marry believed in me and what I could do, and consequently I found I could do more than I realized."

Anne Morrow Lindberg became one of America's most popular authors. She and Charles had a tough, mature love tested by triumph and tragedy alike. They were married forty-seven years before death separated them—a period Anne considered far too short a time!

Let the words of my mouth, and the meditation
of my heart, be acceptable in thy sight, O LORD.
❧ Psalm 19:14 KJV ☙

Two can live as cheaply as one—
if one doesn't eat.

CHARLIE SHEDD writes in *Letters to Karen:* "In our married days at seminary we went often to the warehouses on grocer's row. There was one place where they stacked cans of food clear up to the ceiling. There was, however, this one difference between the cans here and those you see on your grocer's shelves. These had no labels. The sorters had tossed them aside as "damaged," which meant anything from a major dent to some minor flaw. The man who ran the warehouse guaranteed this one thing—there was food in each can. He also claimed that nothing was spoiled, but, as he said, 'For three cents what you gonna lose?'

"Do you know how to tell the difference between peaches and plums by the shake of a can? Well, your mother and I became well nigh infallible as shakers of edibles. Of course, no one is perfect; so we sometimes drew chili for dessert. Thank goodness, we had an icebox and plastic covers were cheap; so, we lived it up and laughed and ate away. In fact, we looked forward to our semi-monthly outing to the can hills."

There is a right time for everything . . .
a time to laugh.
Ecclesiastes 3:1,4 TLB

*Love is what you've been
through with somebody.*

WITHIN seconds after their car was hit head-on, Linda knew from the silence in the back seat of the car that their daughter was either badly injured or dead. In the emergency room, two of Linda's suspicions were confirmed: she was pregnant, and her little girl Madeline was critically injured. The next day doctors advised Mark and Linda to disconnect Madeline's life support. She was brain dead.

Linda had heard the grim statistics about the rate of divorce among couples who had lost a child. So she and Mark promised each other from their hospital beds that they would stick together. Once home, however, they both greatly mourned the loss of their daughter and eventually had to admit they had put Madeline ahead of their relationship. A counselor helped them rebuild the foundation of their marriage. "Every day we work hard at our marriage, paying close attention to the rewards," Linda says. "The truth is that when bad things happen, you learn that the only control you have in life is how you will conduct yourself. . . . I appreciate my family for the people they are. . . . And that brings joy I never imagined I'd feel again."

*It (love) always protects, always trusts,
always hopes, always perseveres.*
1 Corinthians 13:7 NIV

Marriage is a promise that is shared by only two—a vow to love and dream and plan together all through life.

IMAGINE that you are in a mountain cabin high above the tree line in winter. Two heaters heat the cabin—one on each side of the room. Over the course of the evening, after fixing dinner and settling down to read over a cup of steaming hot chocolate, you notice that you have shifted from chair to chair until you are sitting much closer to one of the heaters. The heat from the preferred heater is providing virtually all the heat you need—so much so that you barely feel any radiance from the other heater. Upon comparing the two heaters, you find the one you are now sitting closer to has been wired into the main power source of the cabin and that the other was powered only by a small portable generator, explaining why it is barely giving out heat after several hours of use.

Infatuation and love both seem to burn hotly at the beginning of a relationship. But ultimately, infatuation proves to be weak, as if powered by a portable generator. As time passes, its power and heat fade. Love, however, provides ongoing heat. It maintains its power and eventually, far overshadows anything infatuation offered.

If two of you on earth agree (harmonize together, make a symphony together) about whatever [anything and everything] they may ask, it will come to pass and be done for them.
     Matthew 18:19 AMP

Two souls with but a single thought,
two hearts that beat as one.

A MAN found a wallet in the street one day. There was no identification inside—only three dollars and a crumpled letter with a barely legible return address on the envelope. When he opened the letter, he discovered it had been written some sixty years ago by a woman named Hannah. She was explaining to a man named Michael that her mother wouldn't allow her to see him again, but that she would always love him.

The man set out to find Hannah. He soon located her in a nursing home. She was seventy-six and had never married—there had just never been anyone like Michael. As the man was leaving, the doorman noticed the wallet and said, "That's Mr. Goldstein's. He's one of the old-timers on the eighth floor." The man immediately went to see Mr. Goldstein, now seventy-eight, who told him he had never married—no one had been like Hannah. The man said, "I think I know where she is," and escorted Michael down to the third floor, where he was reunited with his beloved!

Three weeks later, Michael and Hannah married, a perfect ending to a genuine love.

A man shall leave his father and mother and be joined to his wife,
and the two shall become one flesh.

✎ Ephesians 5:31 NKJV ✍

*Spouses who put their
partners first
have marriages that last.*

MIKE MASON, author of *The Mystery of Marriage,* writes that when most people talk about the "work" of marriage, they primarily mean "precious time." He says, "It is like the amount of fuel that must be fed into a big, powerful, shiny, eight-cylinder gas guzzler that has to be kept constantly on the road. You cannot leave a marriage sitting in the driveway even for a day, because the only reason for marriage is togetherness. It is an alliance of love, and love is a spiritual vehicle, a rocket ship, that travels faster and farther than anything else under the sun.

"Get out of it for a moment, and it leaves without you for parts unknown; let it idle, and it begins to rust; neglect it, and it seizes right up. It can be a full-time job just being a passenger in this thing. But like it or not, you and your spouse are in it together, and the work of traveling in marriage is the most vital work you can do. In the Lord's plans for the world there is no work more important than the work of relationship, and no relationship is more important than that of one's marriage."

But in lowliness of mind let each esteem
the other better than himself.
Philippians 2:3 NKJV

Successful marriages usually rest on a foundation of accountability between husbands and wives.

A POPULAR ad slogan in recent years has been, "Together we can do it." That's a good motto to have in marriage. Marriage is a partnership. It is not a matter of one ruling over another, or of two people going their separate ways and occasionally touching base. A partnership means that each person is equally responsible for the whole.

In business, partners rarely are involved in identical activities. One may be in charge of marketing, while the other is in charge of manufacturing. One may manage the finances, while the other manages personnel. Each function, however distinct or visible, is vital to the success of the business. The same is true in a marriage. Each spouse usually has different responsibilities—all of which are vitally important to the success of the relationship.

A business partnership will fail miserably if the partners fail to communicate. They must have goals to which they both agree. They must be able to "create" their business together with a sense of mutual commitment. Again, the same is true for marriage! Communication is a must, and shared goals are what will give hope and life to your relationship.

Together, you can have a marriage partnership.

Submitting yourselves one to another in the fear of God.
❧ Ephesians 5:21 KJV ☙

Be careful that your marriage doesn't become a duel instead of a duet.

HAVE you ever watched puppies and kittens at play? They growl and snarl at each other, and occasionally jump at each other. They seem a constant blur of fur in motion—cuffing at one another, rolling, tumbling, grabbing, chewing, scampering. Puppies and kittens seem to have an endless capacity for rough-and-tumble play.

But occasionally, one in the group will go too far. And that's when "the fur flies." What was once friendly banter turns into serious confrontation and a battle for turf. The growls become a little harsher, the blows are a little harder. The atmosphere changes to one of intensity. Often, the mother dog or cat must step in to break up the scuffle and give the young offenders a sound rebuke.

Most quarrels in marriage begin with just a word or two that goes just "over the line" from banter to badger, from nudge to nag, from comment to criticism. Quarrels nearly always lead to a perceived need for retaliation, justification, and recrimination. They destroy not only the peace between two people but also the inner peace of both parties involved.

Words are a powerful force; choose carefully. They can either calm the nerves or pierce the heart.

Let us therefore follow after the things which make for peace, and things wherewith one may edify another.

Romans 14:19 KJV

You can send your marriage to an early grave with a series of little digs.

A GOLDEN anniversary party was once given in honor of an elderly couple. The husband was moved by the many gestures of love that they had received from their family and friends. He stood to give a toast to his wife, saying, "My dear wife, after fifty years I've found you tried and true!" Everyone smiled approval, but his wife, who was hard of hearing, responded, "Eh?"

He repeated louder, "AFTER FIFTY YEARS I'VE FOUND YOU TRIED AND TRUE!" His wife bristled and immediately shot back, "Well, let me tell you something—after fifty years I'm tired of you, too!"

Little barbs are just that—barbs. They are like the twisted bits of wire found on a barbed-wire fence. While a fence may be a good thing in terms of setting boundaries to a relationship, giving a sense of security and protection, barbs are a reminder that the relationship is one that has pain associated with it. Even teasing that begins in fun can end up being an irritant. So, too, are cutting, cynical, and sarcastic remarks, prickly, unkind comments, and pointed jokes.

Very often the key to improved communication is the removal of barbs and the filling in of "digs."

Death and life are in the power of the tongue: and they that love it shall eat the fruit thereof.
Proverbs 18:21 KJV

Love is the condition in which the happiness of another person is essential to your own.

IN his best-seller, *Maybe (Maybe Not)*, Robert Fulghum tells the story of a couple who had agreed prior to marriage that they would either have children or pets, but not both. Two daughters later, Tom thought their deal was secure until his wife helped organize an auction to raise money for their daughters' school. She planned to use her own expertise in raising dogs as a way of providing a valuable item for the event. So she went to the pound and brought home a puppy, intending to contribute it to the cause.

As soon as the dog had gone on the block, Fulghum writes, "There is a sniffle from the mother. Tears are running own her face and the dog is licking the tears off her cheeks. In a whisper not really meant for public notice, the mother calls to her husband: 'Tom, Tom, I can't sell this dog—I want this dog—I love him—oh, Tom.' Every eye in the room is on this soapy drama. The father feels ill, realizing the great bowling ball of fate is headed down his alley. At that moment, everybody in the room knows who is going to buy the pooch."

[Love] . . . does not seek its own.

☙ 1 Corinthians 13:5 ❧

Being married teaches us at least one very valuable lesson—to think before we speak.

THANK You, God, for teaching us to talk to one another. Thank You for the gift of words.

Thank You for giving us each other with whom to share our hopes, our fears, our problems, and our plans.

Thank You for the assurance, that since there is no fear in love, we can be totally honest, completely ourselves, without the risk of ridicule or rejection.

Thank You for showing us the need to listen. To listen with our hearts as well as with our ears. To sense the needs that may remain unspoken beneath a torrent of words. And to know that when there are no words to meet the situation, love can be a silent song—a touch that says, "I'm in this situation with you," a smile that reassures, "You're doing fine."

Thank You that we have learned the need for patience; the discipline to talk things through until both minds are satisfied, even if we then return to the original solution!

Thank You for teaching a talkative partner brevity, and a quiet one how to express himself.

Thank You, God, for teaching us to talk to one another. Thank You for the gift of words.

—Marion Stroud, The *Gift of Marriage*

A word aptly spoken is like apples of gold in settings of silver.
Proverbs 25:11 NIV

*Let the wife make the husband glad to come home,
and let him make her sorry to see him leave.*

130

A PASTOR once had a man come into his office and say, "I want what my wife has found." The pastor asked, "What do you think it is that she found?" The man replied, "I'm not sure, but whatever it is, it sure has changed her disposition."

This man's wife had been a difficult, demanding person. She had found it excruciating to give without receiving twice as much in return. Her needs kept the family dynamics constantly in turmoil. She could be extremely unpleasant when things didn't go as *she* had planned.

What had happened? She started attending an Enabler's Group in her neighborhood. The women, all members of the same church, opened their hearts to this woman. One day at the end of a meeting she stayed to talk with one of the women about her life. Facing the fact of her rotten disposition she prayed, almost as an experiment: "Jesus, if You are alive as these people say You are, help me to change." The result of that prayer came slowly but surely. She repeated the prayer each morning, and within just a few months, her husband had not only noticed the difference, but wanted the same!

Let each man of you [without exception] love his wife as [being in a sense] his very own self; and let the wife see that she respects and reverences her husband [that she notices him, regards him].

Ephesians 5:33 AMP

The difficulty with marriage is that we fall in love with a personality, but must live with a character.

TO say that Tina's husband was tight with money would have been an understatement. A friend once said to him, "Jack, you can squeeze a penny so hard it cries." Tina, on the other hand, enjoyed an occasional splurge.

After they married, Jack insisted that Tina account for every penny she spent and that she consult him on any expenditure over $5. Eventually she felt such strict control was destroying her sense of fun in life. So she issued Jack an ultimatum: "Give me a household allowance, but don't question my use of a single penny of it."

At first, Jack was frightened to lose control. What if Tina overspent and he had to come up with even more than he had agreed upon? Tina reminded him that she had once managed her own money quite nicely. So Jack agreed to give the new plan a ninety-day trial.

At the end of the three-month period, Jack not only admitted that he enjoyed the surprises Tina brought into their life, but he increased the amount of money he allowed her to manage. And within two years, Jack was giving himself an allowance and turning the rest of their budget over to Tina!

Confess your faults one to another, and pray one for another.
— James 5:16 KJV —

*It doesn't matter who you marry,
for you are sure to find out the next
morning that it was someone else.*

IN *Magnificent Marriage*, Gordon MacDonald writes: "Conflict of a destructive sort breeds quickly if there is an inability to accept our partner as he really is. A dangerous marital game is called 'Why can't you be like?' . . . It can work with effective force from both sides. The wife who knows that her husband is always comparing her appearance with another woman is hurt just as badly as the man who knows that he is being compared with another man who can afford to take his family to Bermuda every spring vacation.

"It was Keith Miller who first made me aware of this fatal cancer of relationship. . . . 'In retrospect, I think Mary Allen's vision of a husband was a perfectly balanced blend of big John Wayne, Jack Parr, and Father Flanagan. But in all honesty, I think my premarital vision of an ideal wife was probably a combination of St. Teresa, Elizabeth Taylor, and Betty Crocker.' . . . Miller formed new depths to their companionship when he learned to love his wife for exactly what she was and not some plastic model of what he wished for her to be."

I will betroth you to me in faithfulness and love, and
you will really know me then as you never have before.
Hosea 2:20 TLB

No man or woman is a failure who has helped hold a home happily together. He who has been victorious in his home can never be completely defeated.

LEWIS SMEDES of Fuller Theological Seminary once shared with a congregation: "May I share with you some reasons why I believe? All good reasons, none of them the really real reason. There's my family. I believe because I was brought up in a believing family. I don't make any bones about that. I don't know what would have happened to me if I had been born in the depth of Manchuria of a Chinese family. I just don't know. I do know that I was led to believe in the love of God as soon as I learned I should eat my oatmeal. We did a lot of believing in our house. Other kids sang 'Jesus loves me this I know, 'cause the Bible tells me so.' I sang, 'Jesus loves me this I know, 'cause my ma told me so.'

"I wasn't alone. You probably heard about a reporter asking the great German theologian, Karl Barth, toward the end of his career: 'Sir, you've written these great volumes about God, great learned tomes about all the difficult problems of God. How do you know they're all true?' And the great theologian smiled and said, 'Cause my mother said so!'"

Blessed is the man whose quiver is full of them;
they shall not be ashamed, when they speak
with their enemies in the gate.
Psalm 127:5

Making marriage work is like operating a farm. You have to start all over again each morning.

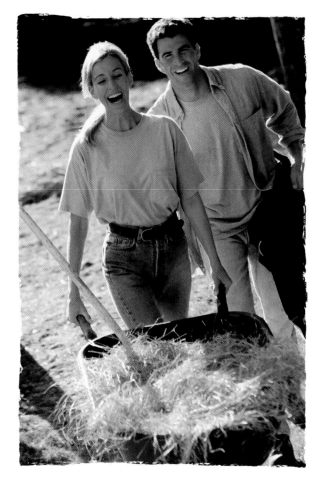

PAMELA, from Europe, met her husband Steve while they were both traveling in Israel. After a romantic, whirlwind courtship, they married. Within three years, Pam found herself living in a small town in the United States, caring for two babies. The hardest part of the transition in her life, however, was the change she saw in Steve. He worked long hours, stayed out late with friends, and did little to help her with the children.

A counselor helped Pam take a look at her own life. She soon recognized that there was a difference in her own behavior in their getting-along times and their times of conflict. In a nutshell, when Pam was nice to Steve, he was nice to her. With this new awareness, Pam set about to change her ways. When Steve came home late, she didn't protest. She simply asked how his day had gone. Before too many days, Pam noticed that Steve was coming home earlier. Then one Saturday, he got up early to take care of the children so she could sleep in. She was thrilled.

If you feel that things have changed, it might be good to ask yourself, "Am I different?"

Cause me to hear Your lovingkindness
in the morning, for in You do I trust.
 Psalm 143:8 NKJV

Married couples who claim they have never had an argument in forty years either have poor memories or a very dull life to recall.

GIVEN the unique intimacies and experiences of marriage, it's no wonder couples face arguments and anger in their relationship. Learning to deal with anger, though, can defuse a potential battleground.

In *Marriage in the Making,* Richard Exley describes the three basic ways we tend to deal with anger: *"Express it*—let it all hang out! . . . I've witnessed the consequences of this flawed strategy on numerous occasions . . . refereed family fights, rescued abused children, and comforted battered wives.

"Repress it—deny your feelings! Pretend that you are not angry at all. People who handle their anger by repressing it subsequently suffer any number of physical and psychological symptoms . . . ranging from a spastic colon, an ulcer, a rash, or even a heart attack.

"The third, and most effective, way of dealing with your anger is to own it. *Confess it*—acknowledge your feelings! Take responsibility for them . . . process them in an appropriate way. . . . Many people have found prayer to be a safe and effective way of expressing their angry thoughts and feelings. Once they tell God how they feel, and why they are angry, their anger is usually under control."

*Faithful are the wounds of a friend, but
the kisses of an enemy are lavish and deceitful.*
Proverbs 27:6 AMP

You keep a lifetime commitment by keeping promises day by day.

CONTRARY to what many people think, rules usually don't limit and prohibit what a person desires to do as much as they provide security for those who live within them. The patterns of behavior, habits, and rituals a couple develops during their marriage provide structure and assurance. They become the "norms" on which both people can count.

Two parents once made a decision to not allow their children to watch any scary movies on television. Then one night while Mom was out shopping, Dad noticed an old black-and-white horror movie in the TV listings that he had enjoyed as a child. The children saw the listing too and remembered that Dad had once told them about the movie. "Please!" they pleaded. "We promise we won't tell Mom."

However, Dad remembered his own promise to Mom, "Your Mom and I agreed on this," he said. "I owe it to her to keep my end of the deal." Not only did Dad keep his children from potential nightmares, he gave them a great lesson in what it means to make a commitment—and keep it.

Keeping the rules of a relationship may very well result in keeping the relationship!

But let your statement be, "Yes, yes" or "No, no;"
and anything beyond these is of evil.
Matthew 5:37

$\mathcal{R}$emember:

The course of true love is full of obstacles.

THE Agassiz brothers lived in a home on the shore of a lake in Switzerland. One winter day, their father was on the other side of the lake and the boys pleaded with their mother to let them cross the lake to join him. Their mother knew the lake was covered with thick ice, so she bundled them up, then stood in their doorway to watch them as they made their way across the ice. She became alarmed when she realized they had come to a crack in the ice. The older boy jumped over the crack easily, but the younger one was afraid. As the mother watched, she saw the older brother get down on his face and stretch his body over the crack to make a bridge. The younger brother slowly crept over him, then the older brother stood and they proceeded safely on their way.

In any marriage, one or the other spouse will encounter a chasm or an obstacle that causes fear. It is in these times that the other spouse must find a way to "bridge the gap"— sometimes enduring hardship and sometimes merely exhibiting lovingkindness—until the two can walk together again in wholeness.

For you have need of endurance, so that after you have done the will of God, you may receive the promise.

Hebrews 10:36 NKJV

The difference between smooth sailing and shipwreck in marriage lies in what you as a couple are doing about the rough weather.

ROGER and Emily had been happily married for fourteen years when tragedy struck: Emily was diagnosed with breast cancer. She underwent extensive chemotherapy, a mastectomy, and then still more chemotherapy. Three years after her ordeal, friends gave Emily a "third-anniversary" party following a yearly series of tests that showed no recurrence of the disease in her life. "Roger was there for me every step of the way," Emily shared with those who had gathered with them to celebrate.

"Were you surprised?" a friend asked jokingly.

"Not at all," Emily said. "But the doctor told me that many husbands are unable to stay with their wives during chemotherapy treatments. Many women come with a female relative or friend. Roger always came with me."

"Was this the worst crisis in your marriage?" another friend asked. "Absolutely," Roger replied. "I couldn't even bear to think that I might lose Emily."

Emily added, "I said earlier that Roger was there for me every step of the way. The point is, we took this as we have taken all things in our marriage: step by step. Some steps are harder than others—but each is still just that, a step."

Just keep stepping!

If thou faint in the day of adversity, thy strength is small.
Proverbs 24:10 KJV

*Married life is a marathon.
It is not enough to make a great start toward
a long-term marriage. You need determination.*

MARATHON runners learn several important lessons over the years. One is that a calamity can happen at any time. No matter how experienced a runner may be, a small stone in the path, a misstep, a distraction, or any other of a myriad of hindrances can occur at any time, breaking the runner's stride and causing an accident or injury. So, too, in marriage. The length of a marriage does not provide immunity from problems.

Marathon runners learn to pace themselves and not to burn themselves out during the first few miles of a race. So, too, couples are wise to see their relationship as one for the "long run" and put all problems and differences into the perspective of a bigger picture.

Finally, marathon runners—with the exception of the handful at the very top of the sport—compete against their own best times. They are not truly in competition with other runners. They run to complete a race and to do *their* best. Competition can ruin a relationship. The far better approach is for each person to work on becoming the best person they can be, and to work on making their relationship the best it can be.

You need to keep on patiently doing God's will if you want him to do for you all that he has promised.

Hebrews 10:36 TLB

*Courtesy costs nothing,
yet it buys things that are priceless.*

WHILE on vacation in New England, Sue and Kevin purchased two red "You're Special" plates at an outlet mall. They liked them so much they decided to use them as their "everyday dishes." Then one day, one of the plates broke. That night, Kevin said, "You should get the special plate tonight."

"Why?" Sue asked.

"Because you finished that big project that you were working on."

The next night, Sue insisted that Kevin dine from the "You're Special" plate, in honor of the help he had given to a neighbor in need. Thereafter, Sue and Kevin vied nightly for the "You're Special" plate honors—not to receive the plate, but for the privilege of awarding it to the other!

When the plate finally broke, Sue said sadly, "I had never been affirmed as much in my entire life as I was these eight months that Kevin and I bestowed upon each other the 'You're Special' honors. What seemed like courtesy the first night that Kevin gave me the plate actually set a precedent for our encouraging each other on a daily basis. We're looking for another set of plates now—including one for the baby that's on the way!"

To sum up, let all be harmonious, sympathetic, brotherly, kindhearted, and humble in spirit.

1 Peter 3:8

You can never be happily married to another until you get a divorce from yourself. Successful marriage demands a certain death to self.

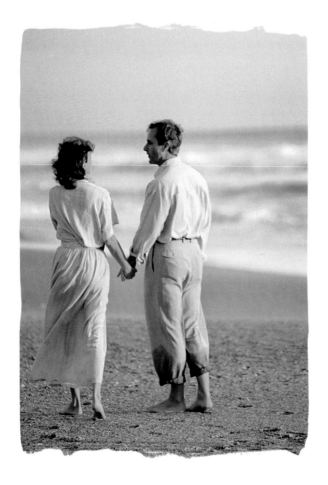

"FROM the moment I met my wife," Mike Mason writes in *The Mystery of Marriage,* "I sensed that a process of interior disintegration was beginning to work in me, systematically, insidiously. In other ways, of course, I was being rejuvenated, tremendously built up. But a thirty-year-old man is like a densely populated city: Nothing new can be built, in its heart, without something else being torn down. So I began to be demolished. There were many times when I felt quite seriously that everything my life had stood for was being challenged, or that somehow I had been tricked into selling my very soul for the sake of a woman's love! . . . There was a lot at stake as the wedding day approached: In fact, there was everything at stake. Later I would discover . . . that that is one of the chief characteristics of love: it asks for everything.

"In marriage the breaking that is done is done by the very heel of love itself. It is not physical pain or natural disaster or the terrible evil world 'out there' that is to blame, but rather it is love, love itself that breaks us."

And they that are Christ's have crucified
the flesh with the affections and lusts.
If we live in the Spirit, let us also walk in the Spirit.
Galatians 5:24-25 KJV

Superfluous wealth can buy superfluities only. Money is not required to buy one necessity of the soul.

THE children of a wealthy family were put into the care of a qualified nanny, as well as a host of other servants the family employed. When adverse market trends impacted the family's finances, the family moved into a slightly smaller home, but they kept the children's nanny. Eventually, however, the family's financial situation became severe enough that they had to let the beloved nanny go.

Then one evening after the father returned home from a day of great anxiety and business worry, his little girl climbed up on his knee and threw her arms around his neck. "I love you, Papa," she said, trying to soothe the weariness she intuitively perceived in him.

"I love you, too, darling," the father replied, glad to have such a warm welcome home. The little girl then said, "Papa, will you make me a promise?" The father said, "What is it?"

So she said, "Papa, please promise me you won't get rich again. You never came to see us when you were rich, but now we can see you every night and hug you and kiss you and climb on your knee. Please don't get rich again!"

Maybe it's time to rethink your priorities.

Wealth is worthless in the day of wrath,
but righteousness delivers from death.
Proverbs 11:4 NIV

Friendship improves happiness, and abates misery, by doubling our joy, and dividing our grief.

A FRIEND is someone you are comfortable with, someone whose company you prefer. A friend is someone you can count on. . . .

A friend is one who believes in you . . . someone with whom you can share your dreams. In fact, a real friend is a person you want to share all of life with—and the sharing doubles the fun.

When you are hurting and you can share your struggles with a friend, it eases the pain. A friend offers you safety and trust. . . . A friend will laugh with you, but not at you . . . a friend is fun.

A friend will pray with you . . . and for you.

My friend is someone with whom I can share my ideas and philosophies, someone with whom I can grow intellectually. . . .

My friend is one who hears my cry of pain, who senses my struggle, who shares my lows as well as my highs.

My friend does not always say I am right, because sometimes I am not. . . . My lover, my friend—this is what a marriage partner should be.

—Colleen Evans

A friend loves at all times, and a brother is born for adversity.
Proverbs 17:17 NIV

If the husband and wife can possibly afford it, they should definitely have separate bathrooms for the sake of their marriage.

GRAMMY-AWARD-WINNING singer, Anita Baker, recently said that one of the secrets to her happy marriage was this: "My husband and I don't hassle each other. . . . I've been very careful to allow him to have his own life, apart from me, and I don't get into his business. If he wants advice, I'll wait for him to ask. If he wants to talk, I try to listen to him instead of telling him, 'Well, if it were my business. . . .' The only thing I will do in terms of involving myself is tell him when it's five o'clock. If he continues working, then I know he needs to.

"As a real estate developer, he's very successful, and I'm really proud of him. I just try to let him have his space and he definitely lets me have mine. So when we come together, it's exciting. I have stuff to talk to him about, he's got stuff to talk to me about, and we definitely have the kids in common. We give each other room to have a life outside of each other."

Giving your spouse "space" may not require separate bathrooms, but having time to call your own.

A happy heart is good medicine and
a cheerful mind works healing.
Proverbs 17:22 AMP

Everyone has an invisible sign hanging from his neck saying, "Make me feel important!"

A TEACHER once asked her group of kindergartners to answer the question, "What is love?" One little girl piped up, "Love is when your mommy reads you a bedtime story." Another little girl quickly added, "And real love is when she doesn't skip any pages."

Every person needs to feel that they are truly acknowledged and made to feel important. But we also need to know this need for recognition is received in different ways. What one person may receive as an expression of approval and appreciation may not be received in the same way by another person. Find out what is meaningful to your spouse. For some, an expression of importance may be the amount of time spent with your spouse or special care given to details. In other cases, your spouse may experience great encouragement from words of praise or gifts of appreciation. In yet other cases, your spouse may feel more important when you go the second mile or do chores that by agreement aren't your own.

Notice things that make your spouse feel special; then make a mental note of it and purpose to do it for them again. Become a student of your spouse.

Therefore encourage one another and build each other up, just as in fact you are doing.
~ 1 Thessalonians 5:11 NIV ~

A thick skin is a gift from God.

JOANNE grew up in a family where friends and relatives freely came and went in each other's homes. They even rummaged through the refrigerator and used the phone without asking. Paul, on the other hand, grew up in a home and neighborhood where each family kept very much to itself. "Making yourself at home" would have been unthinkable to them. You can imagine how appalled Paul was when he walked into his kitchen one morning to find Joanne's nephew searching through the cupboards for an unopened box of cereal! From Joanne's perspective, she just couldn't understand why she had to extend a "formal" invitation before Paul's parents would stop by to visit their grandchildren.

Through the years, Paul and Joanne have adjusted. Paul is still uncomfortable with what seems like a continual stream of people in and out the front door, but he has chosen not to let it interfere with his relationship with Joanne. He just shrugs his shoulders and laughs. Joanne has made it a point to call her in-laws with greater frequency and invite them to their home.

"But mostly," Joanne has said, "we both toughened up a little and decided not to let little differences become big."

A man's wisdom gives him patience; it is
to his glory to overlook an offense.
Proverbs 19:11 NIV

Marriage is like harmony:
two sets of notes for the same song.

PAUL McELROY writes eloquently in *Quiet Thoughts*, "Marriage is the bond that ties two loving hearts together. As each ministers to the other, stands by the other, complements as well as compliments the other, the relationship is made fast like the strands of a rope. Love does not consist of two people gazing fondly into each other's eyes, but in moving together in the same direction. As the maple cannot grow under the shadow of the towering oak, so one helpmate cannot develop under the domination of the other. Husband and wife, like two musicians playing different notes on different instruments, should be able to create harmony as the tones of one blend with those of the other."

A couple was honored with a party on their sixtieth wedding anniversary. The husband, known for being very shy, was asked to share the secret of their long marriage. Unable to speak, he reached for a nearby fiddle and began to play. His wife picked up the tune and began to sing. When the song ended, the wife said simply, "We both know all the same songs. I never sing for any other fiddler, and he never plays for any other singer."

Complete my joy by being of the same mind, having the same love, being in full accord and of one mind.

Philippians 2:2 RSV

*If love is a jigsaw puzzle,
falling in love is finding the corners.*

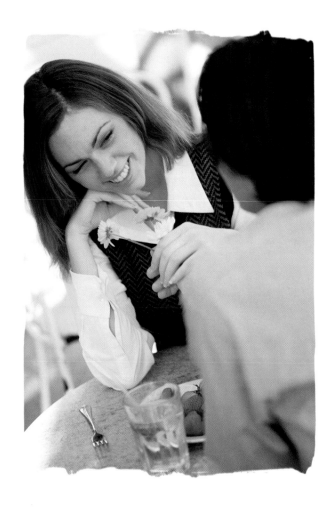

THERE'S very little that is subtle about love, although we like to think of love in soft, gentle terms.

We may say we have "fallen" in love, but in fact, love plummets into our hearts. It seems to come from nowhere. We suddenly feel love beating in our hearts, as if injected into us full strength, without warning.

We may say we are "growing together" in love. In fact, love causes us to collide together as if we were two planets on an overlapping orbit.

We like to speak of the "mystery" of love. But in fact, love is the most real, obvious, and overwhelming emotion any of us will ever feel.

We speak of the lyrical language of love. But most of us are tongue-tied by it and stand silently in awe of it.

We may say we are warmed slowly by love's embrace. But in fact, love usually erupts within us like a volcano, then flows over us so as to incapacitate us from feeling any other emotion.

We may think of love as being fragile. In fact, love is the strongest thing we can ever know—it alone has the power to endure and to remain—forever.

But now abide faith, hope, and love, these three;
but the greatest of these is love.
1 Corinthians 13:13

*May the love you share be as timeless
as the tides and as deep as the sea.*

A GOOD relationship has a pattern like a dance and is built on some of the same rules. The partners do not need to hold on tightly, because they move confidently in the same pattern, intricate . . . swift and free, like a country dance of Mozart's. To touch heavily would be to arrest the pattern and freeze the movement. There is no place here for the possessive clutch, the clinging arm, the heavy hand; only the slightest touch in passing. Now arm in arm, face to face, back to back—it does not matter which. They know they are partners moving to the same rhythm, creating a pattern together, being invisibly nourished by it. . . .

When the heart is flooded with love there is no room in it for fear, doubt, or hesitation. It is this lack of fear that makes for the dance. When each partner loves so completely that he has forgotten to ask himself whether or not he is loved in return; when he only knows he loves and is moving to its music—then, and then only, are two people able to dance perfectly in tune to the same rhythm.

—Anne Morrow Lindberg

Love never ends.

1 Corinthians 13:8 RSV

God gave women a sense of humor—so they could understand their husbands' bad jokes.

CONSIDER the wife of a hard-to-please husband who was determined to try to satisfy him. "What would you like for breakfast this morning, dear?" she asked sweetly.

"Coffee and toast, grits and sausage, and two eggs—one fried, one scrambled," he grumbled. She immediately began cooking, then set before him the meal he requested. Rather than offer her any compliment, however, the man took one look at the plate and said, "I should have expected it. You scrambled the wrong egg."

Or consider the woman who went out for a walk with her husband one afternoon and met friends on their walk. The husband invited the couple back to their house for supper. The wife, too, encouraged them to come, but asked that they wait ten minutes before heading over. She then whispered to her husband, "I'm going to rush over to the deli for a few things. You go home and straighten up." When she returned from her record-setting trip to the deli, she found everything in their home just as they had left it—newspapers strewn about and dishes still in the living room. Her husband was "straightening" the house by changing the light bulb on the back porch!

Husbands, love your wives, just as Christ also loved the church.
— Ephesians 5:25 —

*A good husband should be deaf
and a good wife should be blind.*

A SUCCESSFUL marriage is a give-and-take relationship, with each party doing 90 percent giving, and only 10 percent taking!

Here are ten questions to ask yourself to test your ability to give and take:

1. Are you willing to give silence when your spouse needs a little quiet time?
2. Are you willing to take a rebuke, and let it rest unchallenged?
3. Are you willing to give your spouse the benefit of the doubt?
4. Are you willing to take on the extra chore during a time when you know your spouse is feeling stressed?
5. Are you willing to give a spontaneous word of encouragement?
6. Are you willing to take time to spend with your spouse— alone, without interruption?
7. Are you willing to give your spouse the courtesy of "please" and "thank you"?
8. Are you willing to take a "time out" when a disagreement appears to be overheating?
9. Are you willing to give a compliment?
10. Are you willing to take criticism?

If you couldn't answer yes to all of those questions, take heart. Marriage is a growing process. As each of you grows in your willingness to give and take, you will grow closer together.

Be gentle and ready to forgive; never hold grudges.
Colossians 3:13 TLB

*Straighten your problems out
before you go to bed.
That way you will wake up smiling.*

IN *The Total Woman*, Marabel Morgan gives advice for cooling arguments before a day's end:

1. Control your tears. When I'm mad at Charlie, I warn him ahead of time by telling him, "I'm going to get emotional. Wait a minute." Sometimes I run upstairs, cry, and feel sorry for myself. After I calm down and regain my composure, I return to carry on the conversation. I try not to sulk, nag, or refuse sex as punishment. I find that it's best to say what I have to say, and then forgive and forget.
2. Plan the proper time and atmosphere. Before you speak, think the problem through and put it into its proper perspective. Don't tear into your spouse without thinking, and especially not in public.
3. Gently tell him what is in your heart. The Bible advises us to speak the truth in love. Express your emotions in words, so he'll know what's going on inside you. Your main purpose should be to make your feelings understood, not to demand a change.

You can defer your anger by replacing it with understanding. Confrontation and conflict can bring growth and intimacy to marriage when it is handled in the proper way—with love and undertstanding.

Be angry, and yet do not sin;
do not let the sun go down on your anger.
— Ephesians 4:26 —

A husband should compliment his wife, bring her flowers, and tell her that he cares. These are the ingredients of genuine passion.

MOST of us have heard the old saying, "Women give sex in order to get intimacy. Men give intimacy in order to get sex." We laugh at the play on words, but in truth, men and women seem to want different things from a sexual relationship. One national survey recently showed that 72 percent of the women polled would choose loving closeness and tenderness to sex if they could have only one or the other.

For many men, sex is a matter of primal conquest—of getting what the man needs to meet a physical drive. That drive is rooted largely in what a man sees and senses. For women, sex is a part of romance—of having dreams fulfilled. A woman's approach to sex is based largely in her mind.

Truly to satisfy a partner, each must recognize these differences. A woman is wise to make herself as attractive to her husband as possible. A man is wise to trigger his wife's imagination with genuine compliments and expressions of tender care.

Marriage is a matter of meeting each other's needs; and very often, understanding of those needs must come before a spouse can begin to meet them!

Her children rise up and bless her; her husband also, and he praises her, saying: "Many daughters have done nobly, but you excel them all."

Proverbs 31:28-29

Before criticizing your wife's faults, you must remember it may have been these very defects which prevented her from getting a better husband than the one she married.

A SIX-YEAR-OLD boy was sent home one day with a note from his teacher. The note suggested that the boy be taken out of school since he was "too stupid to learn." The boy was Thomas A. Edison.

A grandfather once gave his grandson ten shillings for writing a eulogy about his grandmother. The grandfather said as he gave him the money, "There, that is the first money you ever earned for your poetry, and take my word for it, it will be the last." The lad was Alfred Tennyson.

A woman once hesitated in letting her daughter marry a printer who had asked for her hand in marriage. She was concerned that the United States already had two printing offices, and she feared the nation might not be able to support a third. The printer was Benjamin Franklin.

So often we fail to recognize the greatness in those with whom we live. It's almost as if we can't see the scope of the person's life because we are standing too close to him or her. Be careful whom you criticize. You may very well be putting down someone whose name will go down in history, even if yours will not.

Therefore let us not judge one another anymore,
but rather determine this—not to put an obstacle
or a stumbling block in a brother's way.

Romans 14:13

*The most successful marriages are those
where both the husband and the wife
seek to build the self-esteem of the other.*

JOHNNY lived in the South Pacific, where all the islanders spoke highly of him. He was seeking a wife and the normal custom was for a man to obtain a wife by paying her father in cattle. Four to six cows was considered a high price. Johnny chose a plain, skinny young woman who walked with her shoulders hunched over and her head down. Yet, he offered her father eight cows!

People laughed at Johnny in disbelief.

A visitor arrived in Johnny's village several months later and heard the story of Johnny's eight-cow wife. When he saw Johnny and met his wife, the visitor was extremely surprised. He didn't see a shy, plain, hesitant woman, but rather, a very beautiful, poised, and confident woman. When Johnny saw the visitor's surprise, he said, "I wanted an eight-cow woman. When I paid eight cows for her and began to treat her like an eight-cow woman, she began to believe in herself as an eight-cow woman. She discovered she was worth more than any other woman on the islands. What matters most is what a woman thinks about herself."

Therefore encourage one another, and build up one another.
∾ 1 Thessalonians 5:11 ∾

*Stack every bit of criticism
between two layers of praise.*

IN *How to Change Your Spouse*, Norman Wright tells about an incident that happened early in his marriage: "I was fairly sloppy when it came to hanging up my pajamas in the morning. I took care of most of my other clothes, but in the morning when I took off my PJ's, I gave them a fling toward a hook in the closet . . . or else they stayed on the bed.

"One day when I was seated on the couch reading the newspaper, Joyce sat down next to me and waited until I turned toward her. I noticed that my pajamas were neatly folded on her lap. She put her arm around me, looked me in the eye and said, 'Norm, I just know that a man of your organizational ability and your attention to detail and results would have such a sense of satisfaction going to work each day knowing that your pajamas were hanging neatly on the closet hook. Thank you for listening.' And with that she walked out of the room leaving me with my mouth hanging open. I didn't even realize until a couple of months later, that since that day, I had been hanging up my pajamas."

Correct, rebuke and encourage—with
great patience and careful instruction.
2 Timothy 4:2 NIV

Of all the home remedies, a good wife is best.

A GROUP of girls were gathered together one rainy afternoon. One of them opened the door for a moment, and as she did, a wave of sweet aroma filled the room.

The girl at the door turned and said to her friends, "Can you smell the sweetbrier down by the gate?" The girls nodded. She added, "It's always fragrant, but never so fragrant as when it rains."

Then one of the girls in the room said impulsively, "It reminds me of my aunt." The other girls giggled slightly and one asked, "Why would you say that?"

The girl explained, "So many flowers are fragrant—just look, this garden has dozens of rose bushes, and their roses are sweet-smelling. But the sweetbrier is the only other plant with fragrant leaves. Everything my aunt does—not just the large things, but the common, everyday things—including the leaves as well as the blossoms—has something beautiful in it. There is a gentleness in her spirit, a thoughtfulness, a graciousness that goes out in everything she does and in every word she speaks."

A spouse who makes each small moment in life special helps all of life to take on a new wonder.

He who finds a wife finds a good thing,
and obtains favor from the LORD.
Proverbs 18:22 NKJV

*A woman must be a genius
to create a good husband.*

IN *A Time for Remembering*, Ruth Bell Graham writes that when she was a teenager, leaving her childhood home in China for schooling in Korea, she fully intended to be an old maid missionary to Tibet. She did, however, give some thought to the particulars that she would require in a man if she could ever be persuaded to marry. She wrote in her diary:

"If I marry: He must be so tall that when he is on his knees, as one has said, he reaches all the way to heaven. His shoulders must be broad enough to bear the burden of a family. His lips must be strong enough to smile, firm enough to say no, and tender enough to kiss. Love must be so deep that it takes its stand in Christ and so wide that it takes the whole lost world in. He must be big enough to be gentle and great enough to be thoughtful. His arms must be strong enough to carry a little child."

Did Ruth Bell find such a man in Billy Graham? Perhaps not as much on the day she met him, as on the day they celebrated their fiftieth wedding anniversary.

She opens her mouth in skillful and godly Wisdom,
and on her tongue is the law of kindness.
Proverbs 31:26 AMP

*Success in marriage is more
than finding the right person.
It's also a matter of being the right person.*

MANY women today are weary of trying to be "superwoman"—super mom, super wife, a super professional on the job. They are coming to the realization that a woman may be able to "have it all," but probably not all at the same time! Men, too, are struggling with a "must be perfect" syndrome that seems to pervade our culture.

Rather than try to live up to the world's definition of success, we are wise to discover what it means to be successful in God's eyes, which is being the person *He* created you to be.

This does not mean we should settle for second best in our lives, or fail to develop our talents. What it *does* mean is that each person is free to pursue what it is the Lord calls and directs him or her to do at any point in their life and to express themselves in unique and creative ways.

A woman named Kate had this perspective when she told a reporter who asked her about her life: "I've had nine jobs: waitress, clerk, personnel manager, student, nurse, wife, mom, nursing administrator, and teacher in a nursing school. But I've had only one personality: Kate."

And just as you want people to treat you,
treat them in the same way.
Luke 6:31

Everyone has patience.
Successful people learn to use it.

IN *Traveling Hopefully,* Stan Mooneyham writes, "Early on I learned that it is a lot more fun to harvest than to hoe. Or, for that matter, to plant. Few rewards can compare with that of plucking the bounty of the earth, which represents the fruit of your labor. Harvesting is dramatic, fulfilling. You see what you get and you get what you see.

"Not that harvesting isn't hard work, too; but it's different. That's the payoff. The sense of reward represented by autumn's harvest can cause you to forget the less satisfying work of spring and summer. . . .

"Of course, it goes without saying that there would be no autumn harvest if there was no drudgery of spring and summer. Full barns require soil preparation, planting, and hoeing. The 'winning run' in baseball may top off all the prior runs, but the first was as necessary as the final one, even if the crowds didn't leap to their feet and tear the stadium apart early in the game."

If you find yourself feeling that marriage has turned into drudgery and work, consider the possibility that life has a wonderful reward ahead. You may not see it today, but that reward is growing!

But let patience have her perfect work,
that ye may be perfect and entire, wanting nothing.
James 1:4 KJV

Love doesn't make the world go 'round.
Love is what makes the ride worthwhile.

"MY husband had come home on the late bus from Lausanne one evening when a couple had come to have me talk to them about marriage," writes Edith Schaeffer in *What Is a Family?* "What to do? My solution was to explain, as I stopped to prepare a tray, that I felt there were priorities to be observed in married life, and that right then a very attractive meal was important. 'See how quickly I can prepare a salad with a round of pineapple on lettuce, a split banana, this orange cut in slices, a piece of cheese, some nuts on top—and this omelet! Now I'll top it off with a small pot of tea, this piece of cake, and a candle in this brass candlestick. . . . Frank will be happier by far to have me talking to you, once he has had his supper, and I have spent a bit of time talking to him. I'll see you in a half an hour.'

"Then I took up the tray and spent time with Frank as he ate in our bedroom. . . . The reality of that object lesson probably would remain in the couple's memory longer than much of what I would later be saying."

There are three things that remain—faith, hope,
and love—and the greatest of these is love.
1 Corinthians 13:13 TLB

You have a lifetime to enjoy one another.
Don't waste a day of it.

194

IN an article in the *Los Angeles Times*, Ann Wells wrote: "My brother-in-law opened the bottom drawer of my sister's bureau and lifted out a tissue-wrapped package. . . . He discarded the tissue and handed me the slip. It was exquisite—silk, handmade, and trimmed with a cobweb of lace. The price tag with an astronomical figure on it was still attached.

"'Jan bought this the first time we went to New York, at least eight or nine years ago. She never wore it. She was saving it for a special occasion. Well, I guess this is the occasion.'

"He took the slip from me and put it on the bed with the other clothes we were taking to the mortician. His hands lingered on the soft material for a moment, then he slammed the drawer shut and turned to me.

"'Don't ever save anything for a special occasion. Every day you are alive is a special occasion.'

"I'm still thinking about his words, and they've changed my life. . . . I'm not 'saving' anything; we use our good china and crystal for every special event—such as losing a pound, getting the sink unstopped, the first camellia blossom."

Live happily with the woman you love
through the fleeting days of life.
~ Ecclesiastes 9:9 TLB ~

In trying times, don't quit trying.

TAKE any major individual-oriented athletic event, and you'll probably find that far more people are starters than are finishers. How many people have started the Tour de France bicycle race, the Boston Marathon, or a swim of the English Channel . . . only to drop out before reaching their goal?

Those who finish these long-distance endurance events speak of "pushing through the wall." The "wall" in these events is the point where the body cries out to the mind, *We can't go on. I've given all I can. I don't have any more to give.* Every endurance racer hits this wall, including those who are in top shape and those who may have completed the event in years past. Those who push through the wall are those whose *mind* says back to their *body, Oh, yes we can.*

This ability to keep moving when your instincts say otherwise is called *perseverance.* Every couple needs to keep that word in mind when they hit the "wall" in their relationship. Perseverance is the ability to hang on. It's the ability to keep going, rather than to call it quits. It's a matter of the heart saying to the relationship, *Oh, yes we can.*

And let us not grow weary in well-doing,
for in due season we shall reap, if we do not lose heart.
Galatians 6:9 RSV

People in love want what's best for each other.

A MAN who had once worked as a general contractor for a large development company suddenly found himself the victim of "downsizing." He quickly put out his resumé, but without success. For the next year, he painted the house, carpooled the children, did the grocery shopping, and generally felt miserable and depressed.

His wife continued to work full-time as a teacher. But her salary alone couldn't support the family. Their savings became sorely depleted. Then the grades of their teenage son began to drop dramatically, and the mother insisted the family enter counseling. She said, "I insisted the counseling was for me, although it was really for my husband and our son. It was all very helpful and we made it." The man went back to school to prepare for a new career. And when the son saw dad returning to school, he studied harder.

Counselors have found that the couples who make it through job-loss crises are usually ones in which the "strong" spouse—the one whose self-esteem is still intact—seeks out what is *best* for the wounded spouse. If your spouse has been wounded in some way, think about what you can do to show that you believe in your spouse.

Love bears all things, believes all things,
hopes all things, endures all things.
1 Corinthians 13:7 RSV

*Marriage takes commitment;
all good things do.*

IN *The Hungering Dark*, Frederick Buechner writes eloquently: "The reality of the bride and groom, which is also their joy, is of course that they love each other; but whereas sentimentality tends to stop right there . . . candor has to move on with eyes . . . to see through. They love each other indeed, and in a grim world their love is a delight to behold, but love as a response of the heart to loveliness, love as primarily an emotion, is only part of what a Christian wedding celebrates, and beyond it are levels that sentimentality cannot see.

"Because the promises that are given are not just promises to love the other when the other is lovely and lovable, but to love the other for better or for worse . . . and that means to love the other even at half-past three in the morning when the baby is crying. The love that is affirmed at a wedding is not just a condition of the heart but an act of the will, and the promise that love makes is to will the other's good even at the expense sometimes of its own good—and that is quite a promise."

So guard yourself in your spirit, and
do not break faith with the wife of your youth.
 Malachi 2:15 NIV

When Adam was lonely, God created for him not ten friends, but one wife.

A NEW wife nagged her husband about not overeating and losing ten pounds. When she finally realized her nagging wasn't motivating him but was hurting him, because he didn't feel accepted by her, she changed her tactics. She began to prepare low-fat meals, with only two servings. She never brought home junk food. And she encouraged her husband to join a gym with his friends. The result was that her husband not only lost weight, but maintained his weight loss.

This same woman also gave careful thought to her husband's education. He had worked full-time during his college years and thus hadn't finished his degree. When he was considering a potential job change, he felt that he wasn't very marketable. So she helped him research degree programs designed for working people. Then once he decided on a program, she brainstormed ideas with him, helped with library research, quizzed him at test time, and typed his papers. He graduated with honors.

Was this woman trying to "make" her husband into something he wasn't? "No," she insists. "These were things my husband both wanted and was capable of doing. We were building a future together. What I did to help *him* ultimately helped us."

A wife of noble character who can find?
She is worth far more than rubies.
Proverbs 31:10 NIV

203

*Family . . . was God's idea, and
He does not make mistakes.*

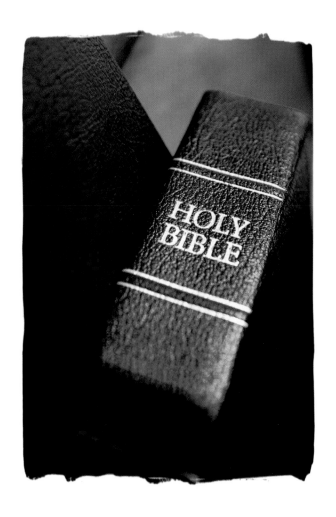

AN old minister once said, "A couple that tries to build a good marriage without God's Word is like someone trying to sit on a three-legged stool that has one leg missing."

The couple who depends on Scripture for solutions to problems they encounter has a distinct advantage over the family with no faith. The Bible is a "window," of sorts, into the mind of the Heavenly Father. It tells us how and why the Creator established marriage and the family, and gives us all the principles necessary for a long, lasting, and loving relationship with another person—with very practical advice on everything from sexual attitudes, to handling money, to disciplining children. The Bible is the ultimate "Handbook on Marriage."

It's not enough, however, for a couple to merely read Scripture. They must also pray and ask God for the wisdom and courage to apply to their lives the truth that they discover. They must live out God's Word in their daily activities—in all they say and do. Only then can the Bible have real meaning and impact upon their marriage.

Perhaps the greatest treasure any family can ever have is a well-worn family Bible.

For this cause a man shall leave his father and his mother,
and shall cleave to his wife; and they shall become one flesh.
Genesis 2:24

Acknowledgments

We acknowledge and thank the following people for the quotes used in this book: Joseph and Lois Bird (6), James Dobson (8,28,120,176,180,194), H. Norman Wright (20), Dan Bennett (26), Margaret Fuller (30), Mae West (32), Charles Meigs (36), Richard Dobbins (38), Margaret E. Sanger (48), Thomas A'Kempis (50), Martin Luther (52), Winston Churchill (56), Mignon McLaughlin (62), Ogden Nash (66), Grit (70), George Eliot (76), Lady Bird Johnson (78), Bishop Jeremy Taylor (92), Lucretius (96), Katherine Ann Porter (100), Heine (102), Andre Maurois (108), James Thurber (112), Maria Lovell (116), R. A. Heinlein (126), Peter Devries (132), Samuel Rogers (134), Robert W. Burns (136), Howard and Jeanne Hendricks (146), Jerry McCant (152), Joseph Addison (156), Doris Day (158), Mary Kay Ash (160,182), Konrad Adenauer (162), Louis Fromm (174), Kin Hubbard (184), Balzac (186), Ignacy Paderewski (190), Franklin P. Jones (192).

Additional copies of this book are available
from your local bookstore.

Also look for these titles from Honor Books:

God's Little Devotional Book—Special Gift Edition
God's Little Devotional Book for Women—Special Gift Edition
God's Little Devotional Book for Women
God's Little Devotional Book for Men
God's Little Devotional Book for Moms
God's Little Devotional Book for Dads

Honor Books
Tulsa, Oklahoma